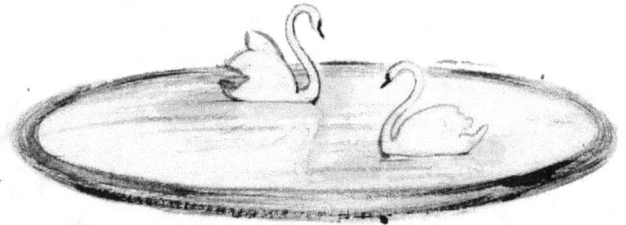

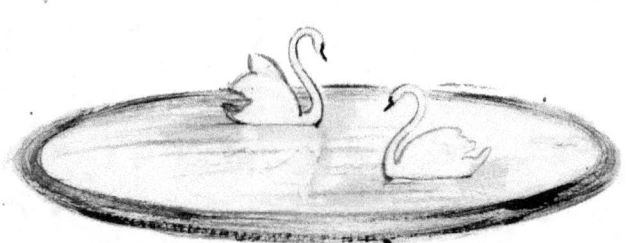

Elena Abdulaeva

Andersen's
Famous
Fairy Tales

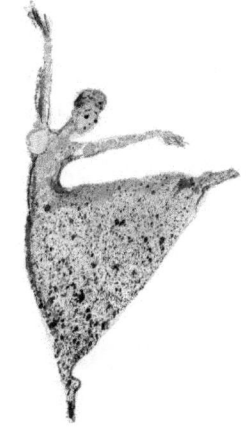

Grayscale Coloring Book

Elena Abdulaeva
Andersen's Famous Fairy Tales
Grayscale Coloring Book

Series of Illustrations by Elena Abdulaeva
Pencil, Acrylics, Watercolor on Paper, 2015
Scanned from Paper Originals, 2016
Processed into Grayscale & Adapted for Coloring, 2017

Published by Elena Abdulaeva, www.abdulaeva.com.
Printed by CreateSpace, an Amazon.com company.
Available at Amazon.com and other retailers.

Fine Art Prints available at art.abdulaeva.com

ISBN-13: 978-1543142518
ISBN-10: 1543142516

The Princess on the Pea

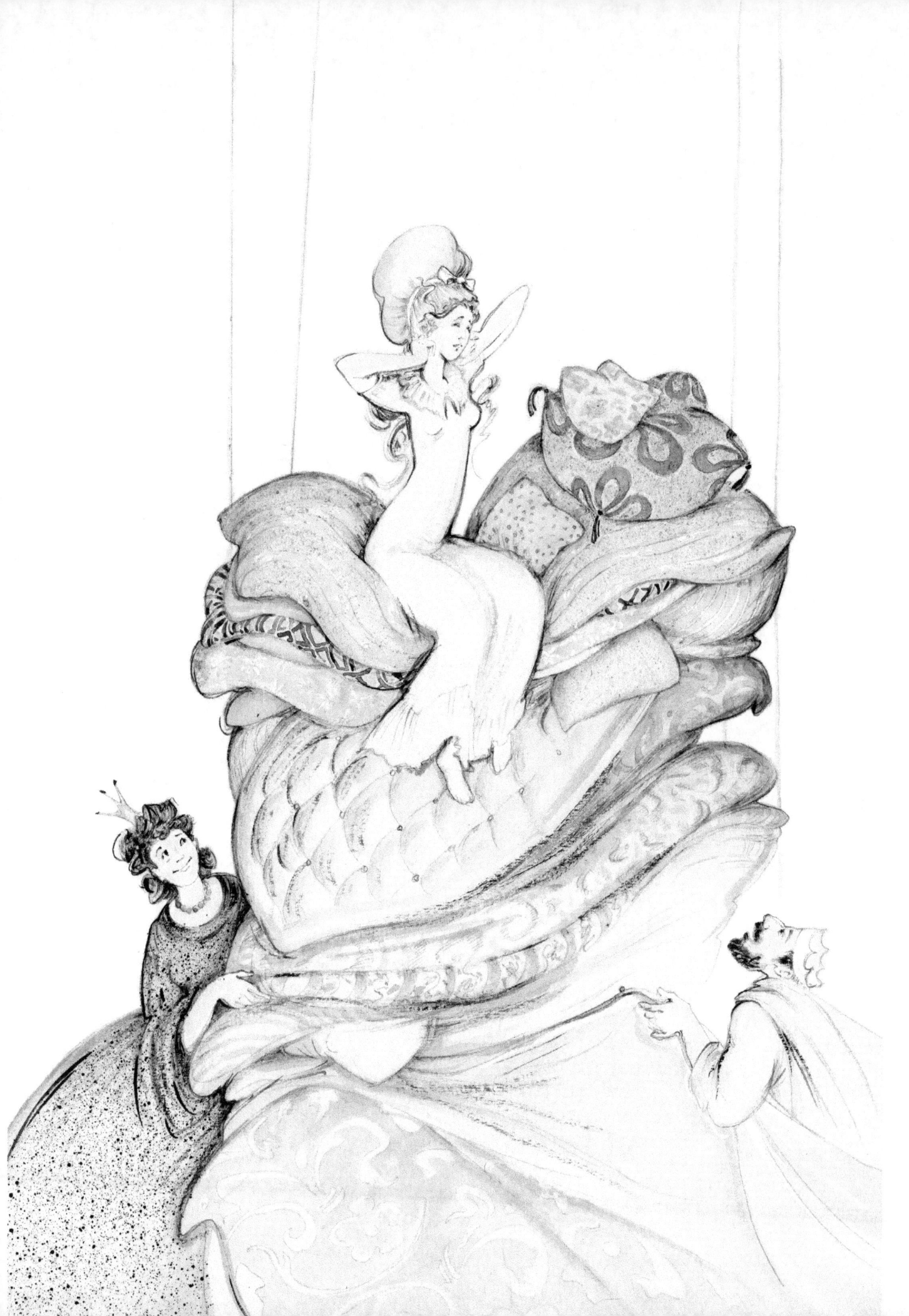

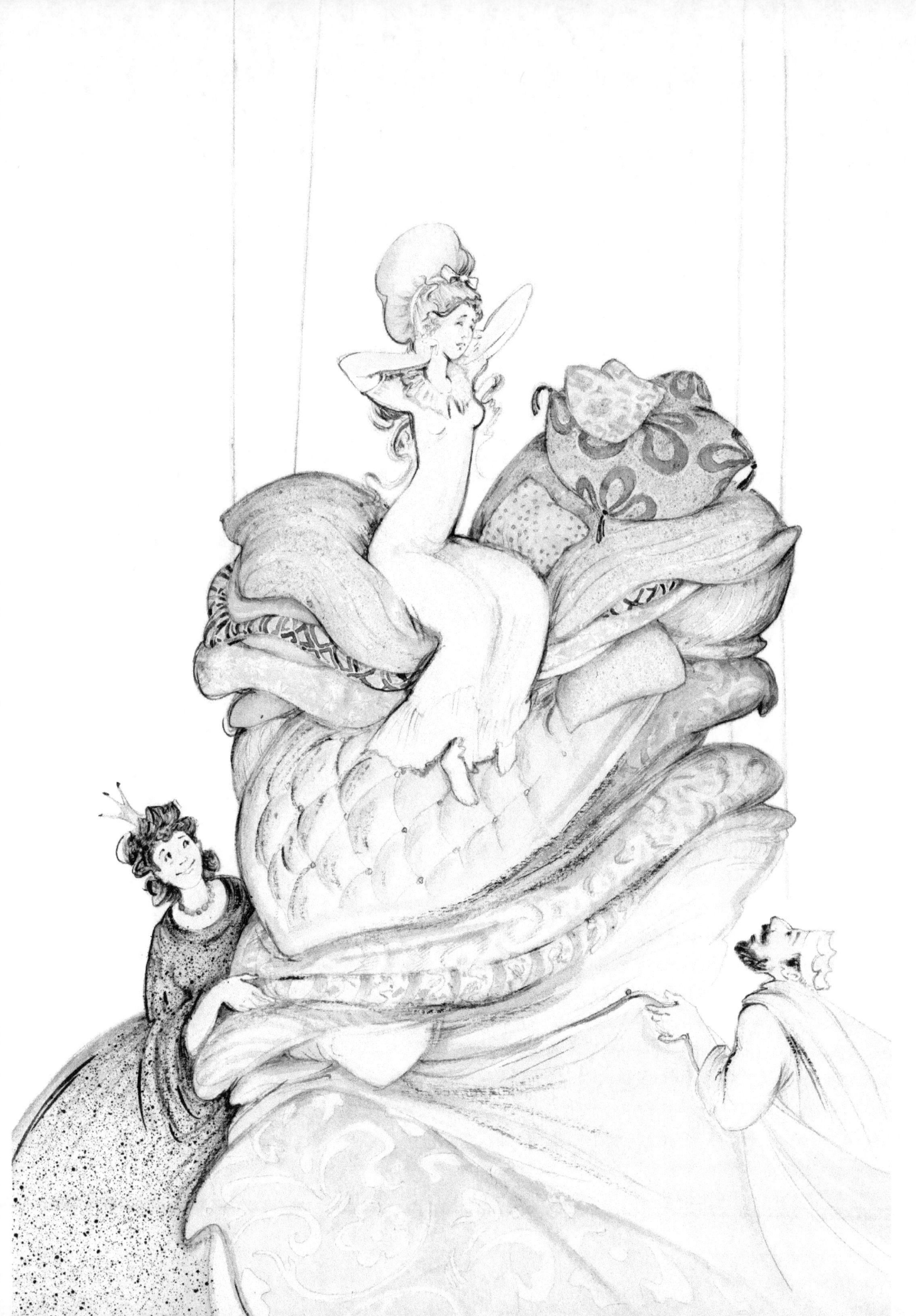

The Ugly Duckling

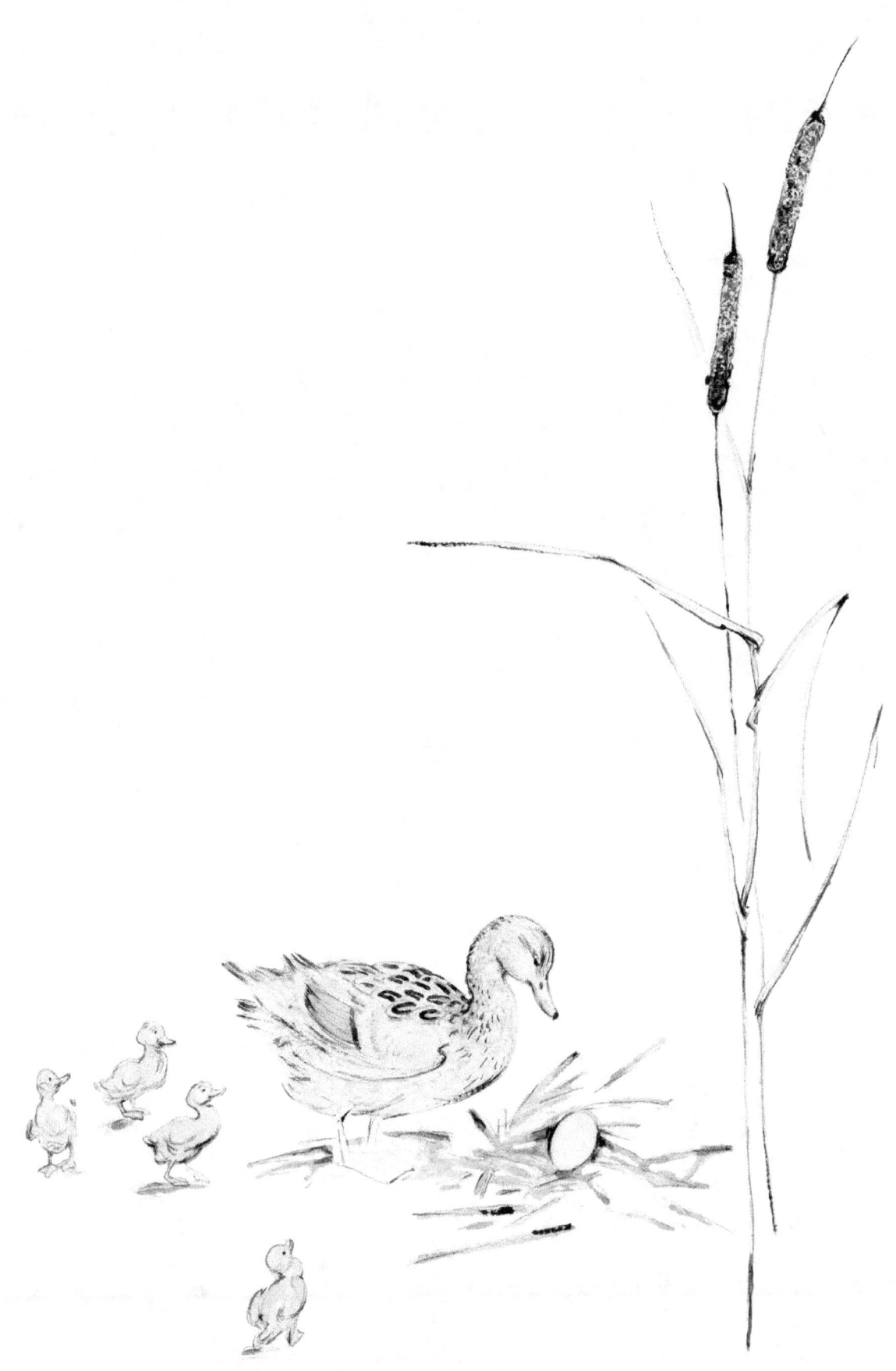

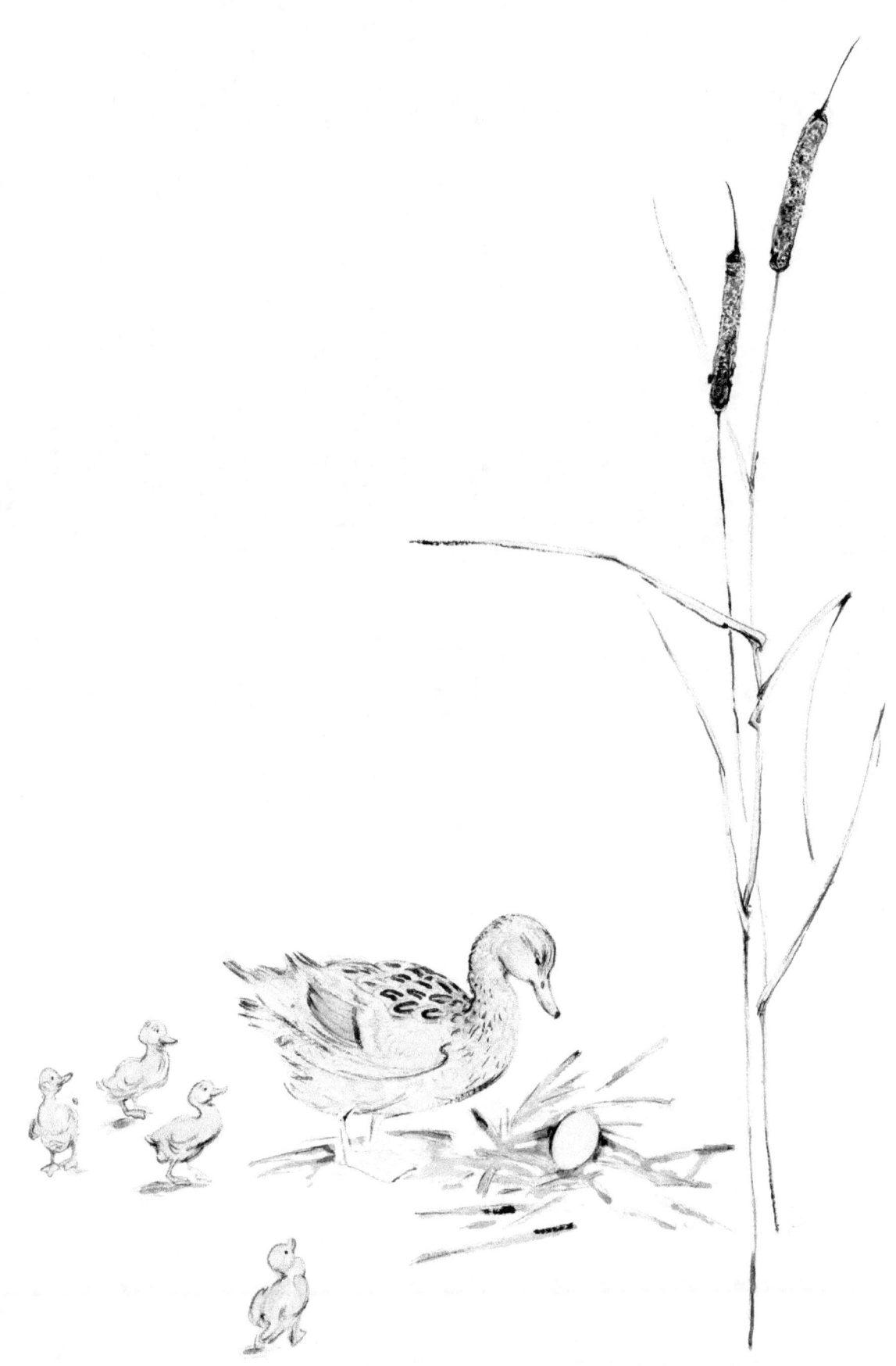

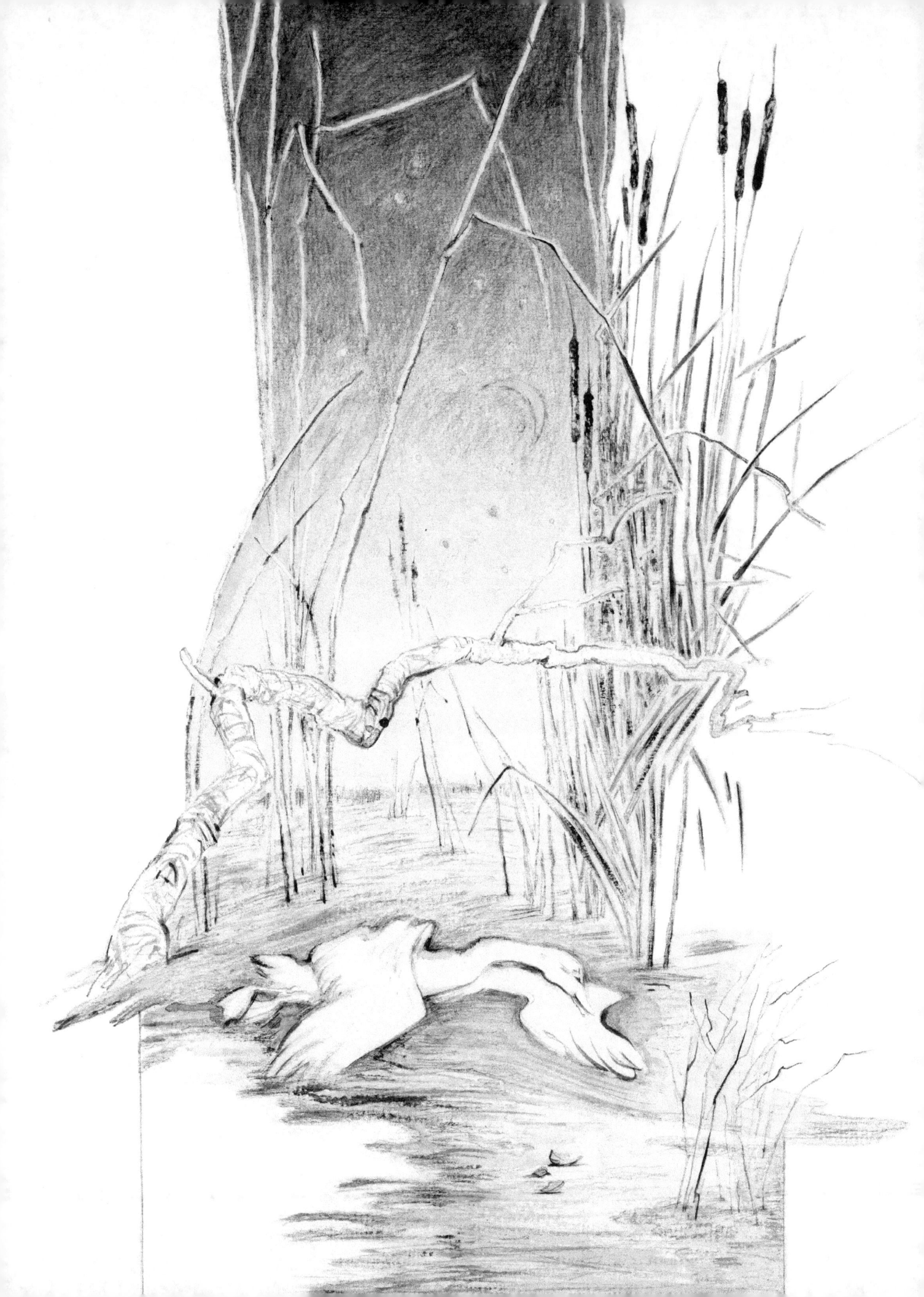

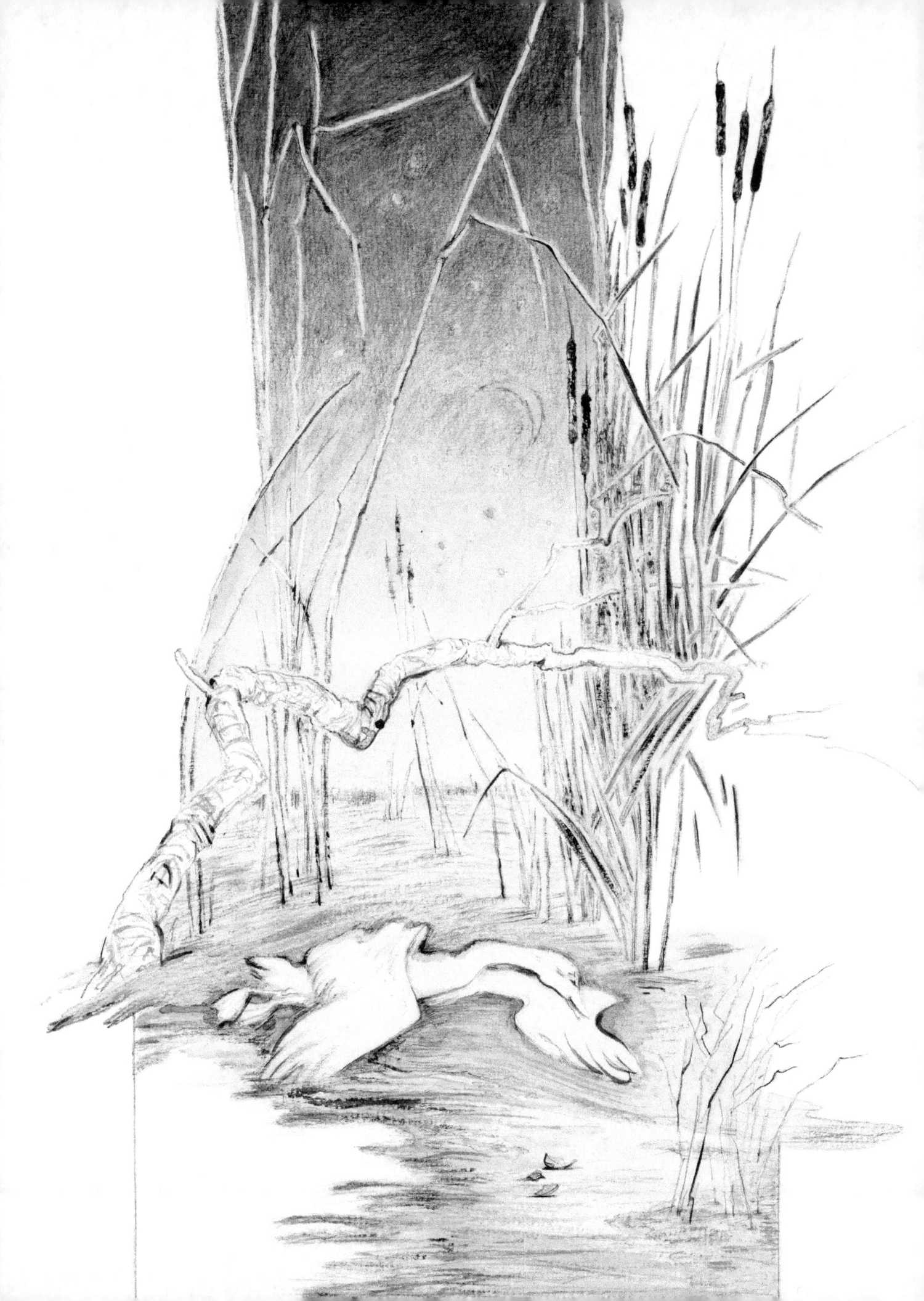

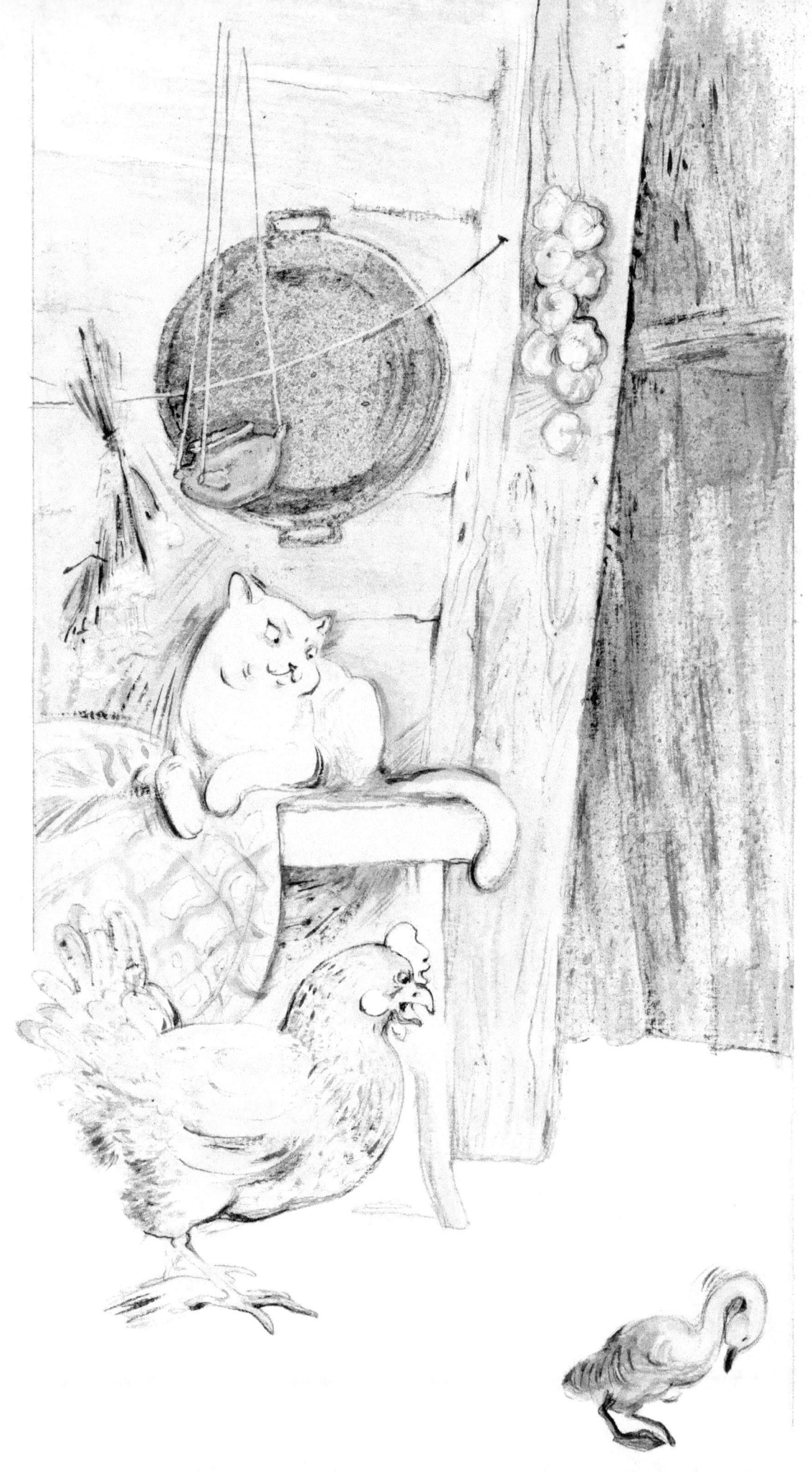

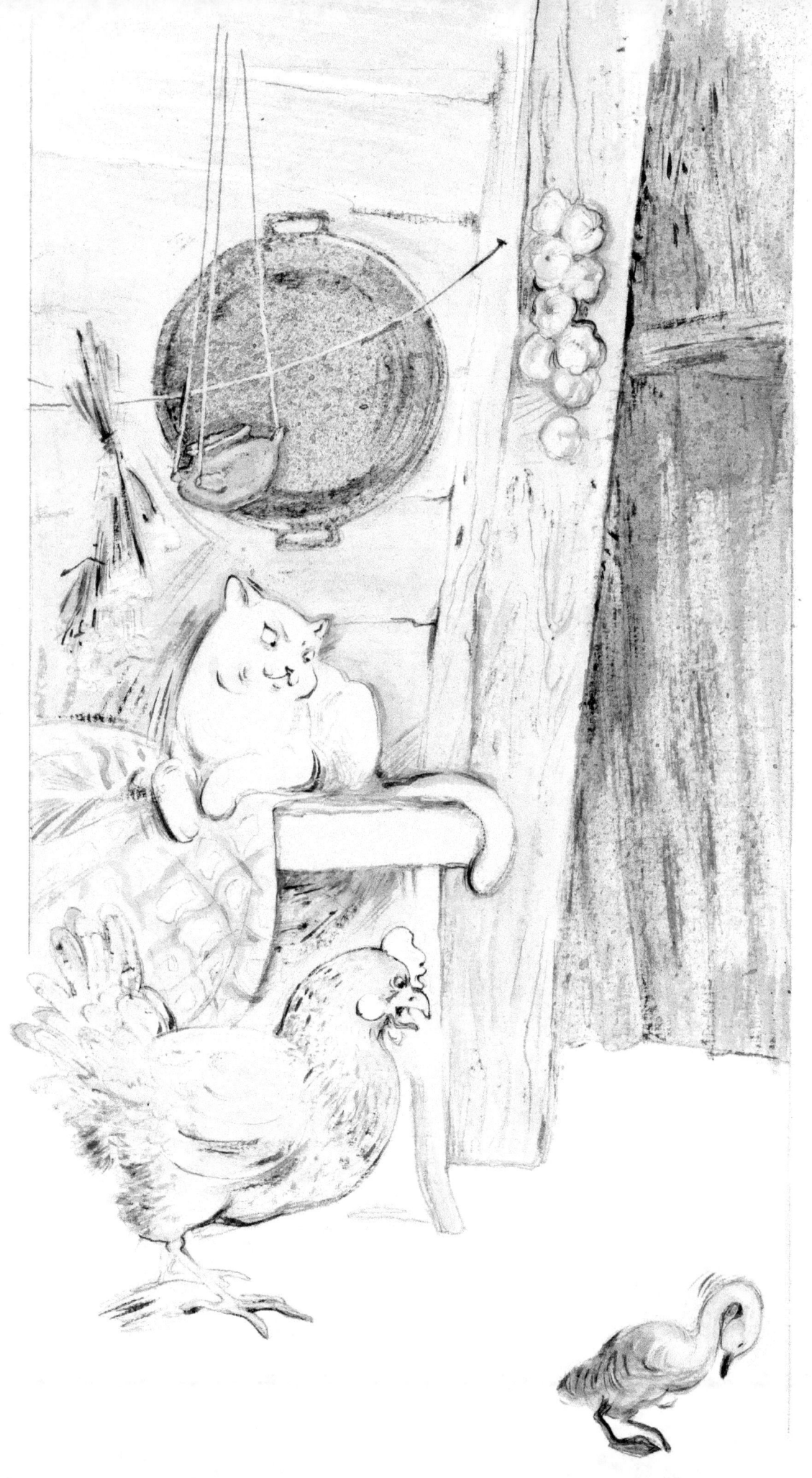

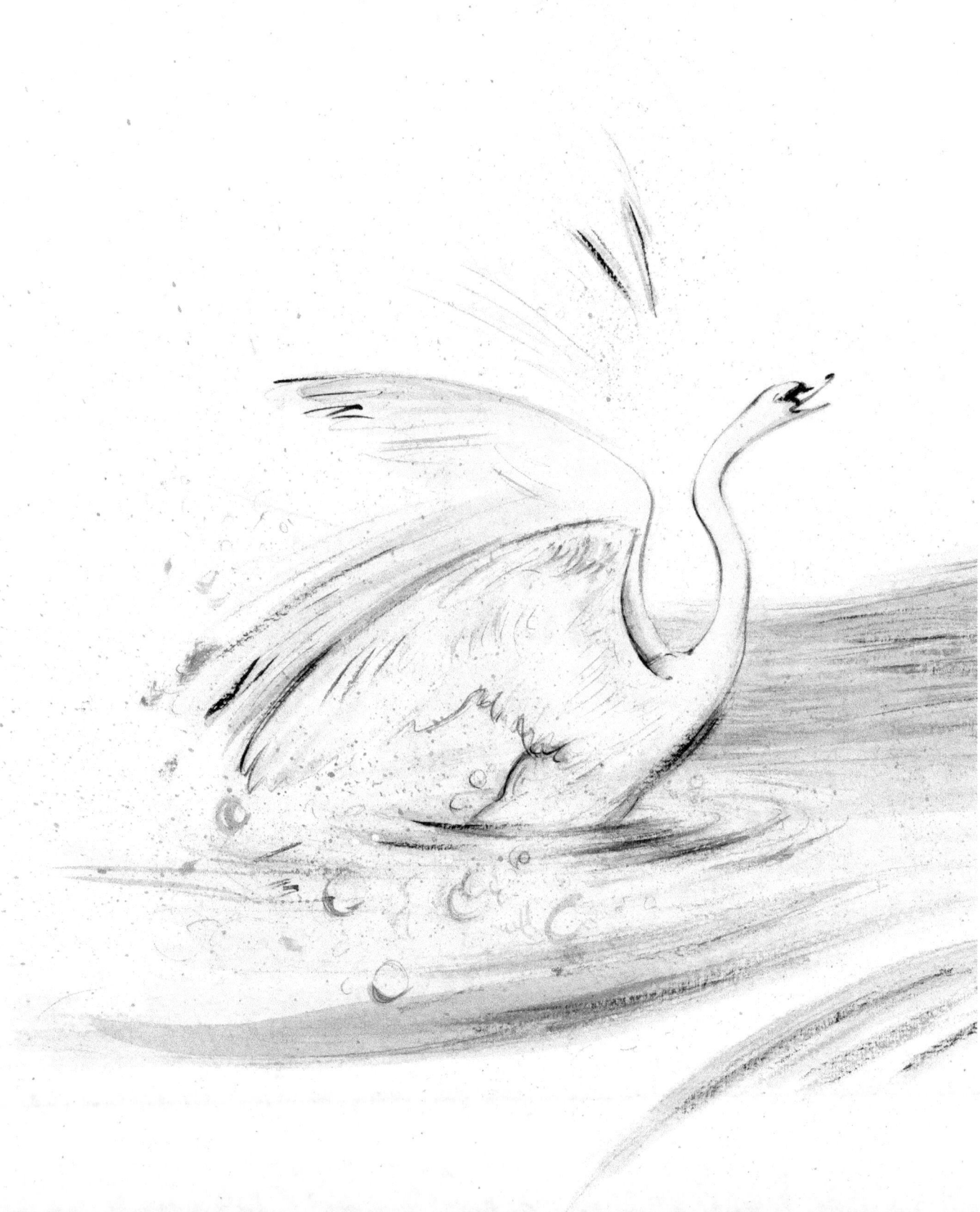

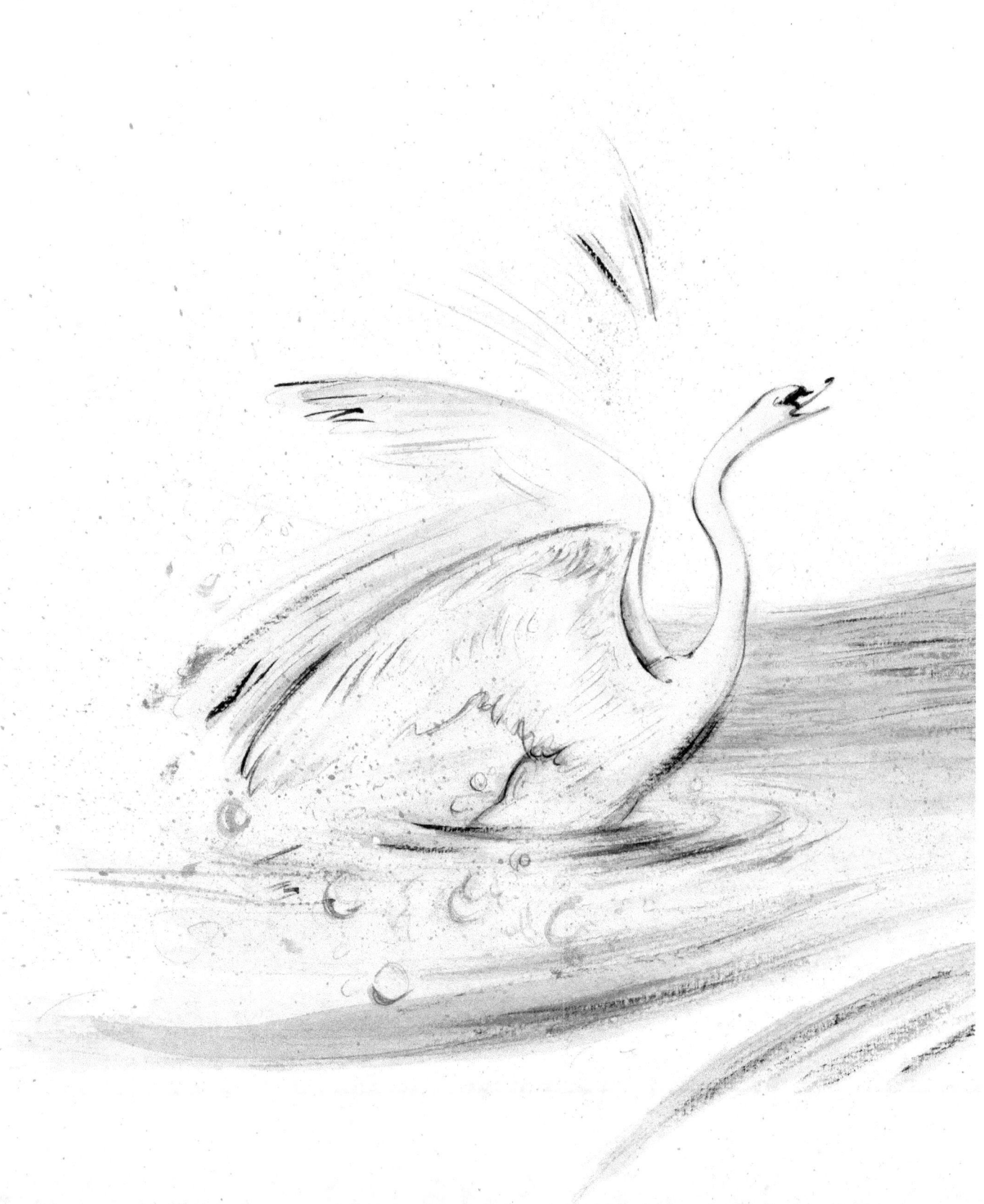

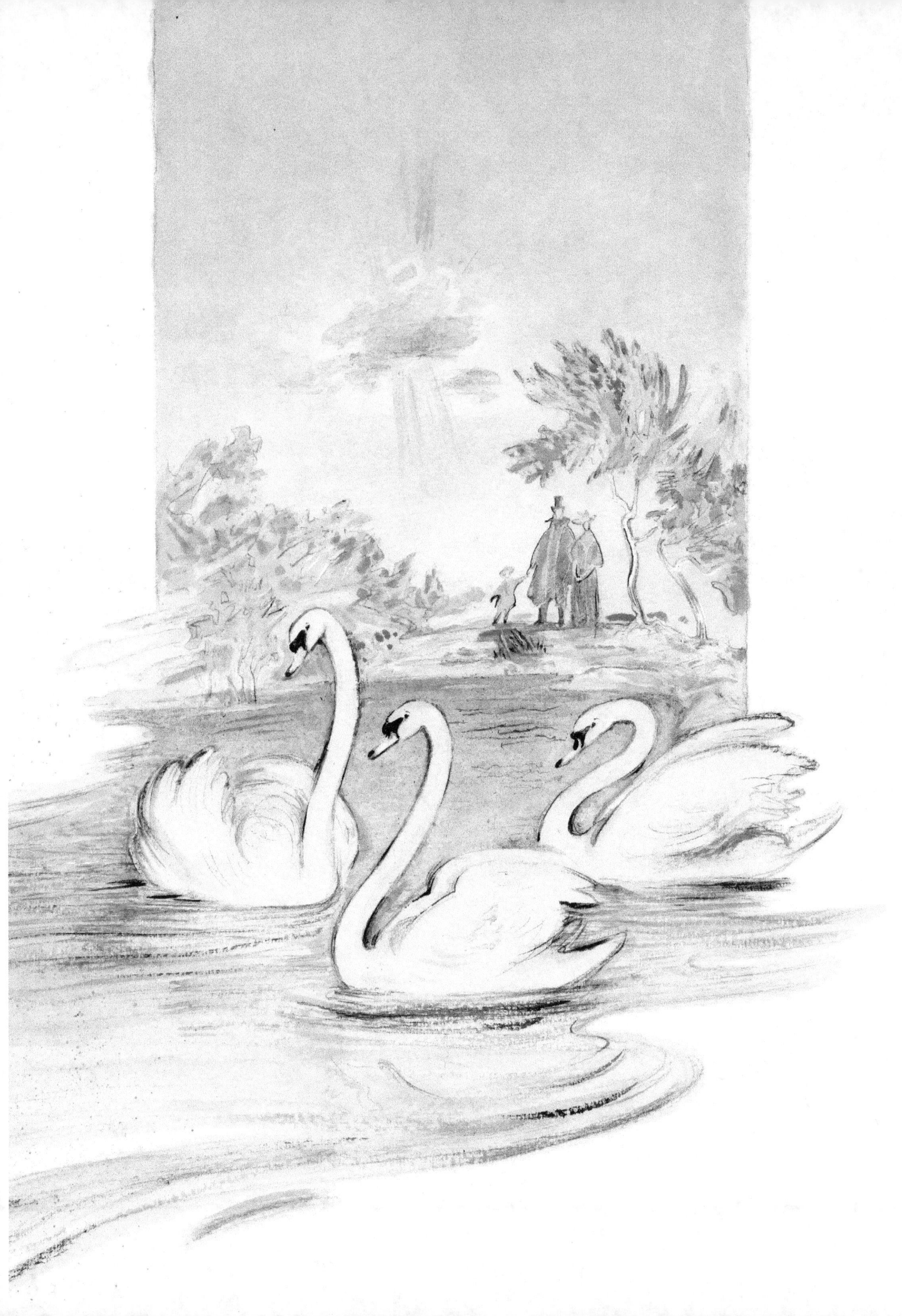

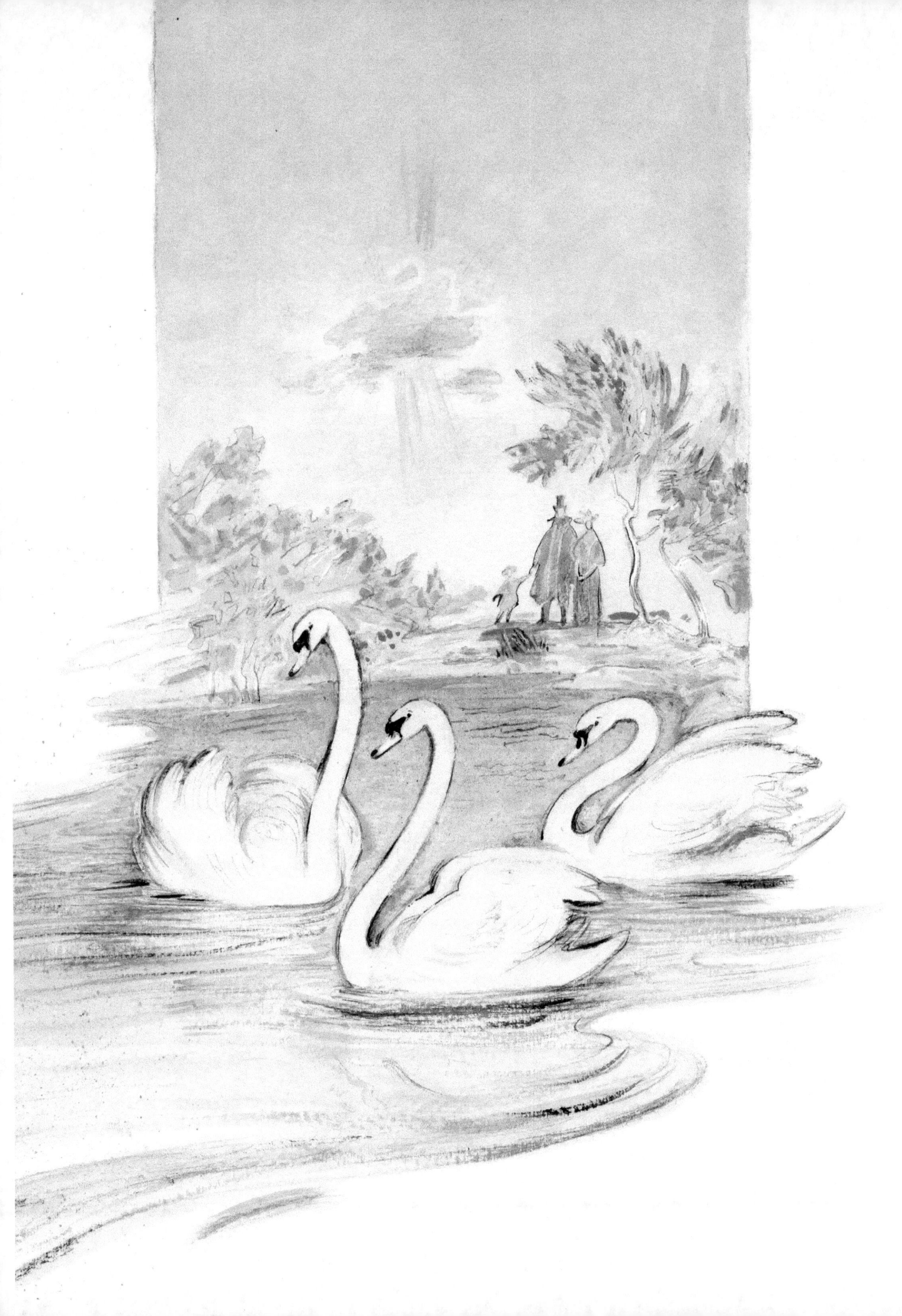

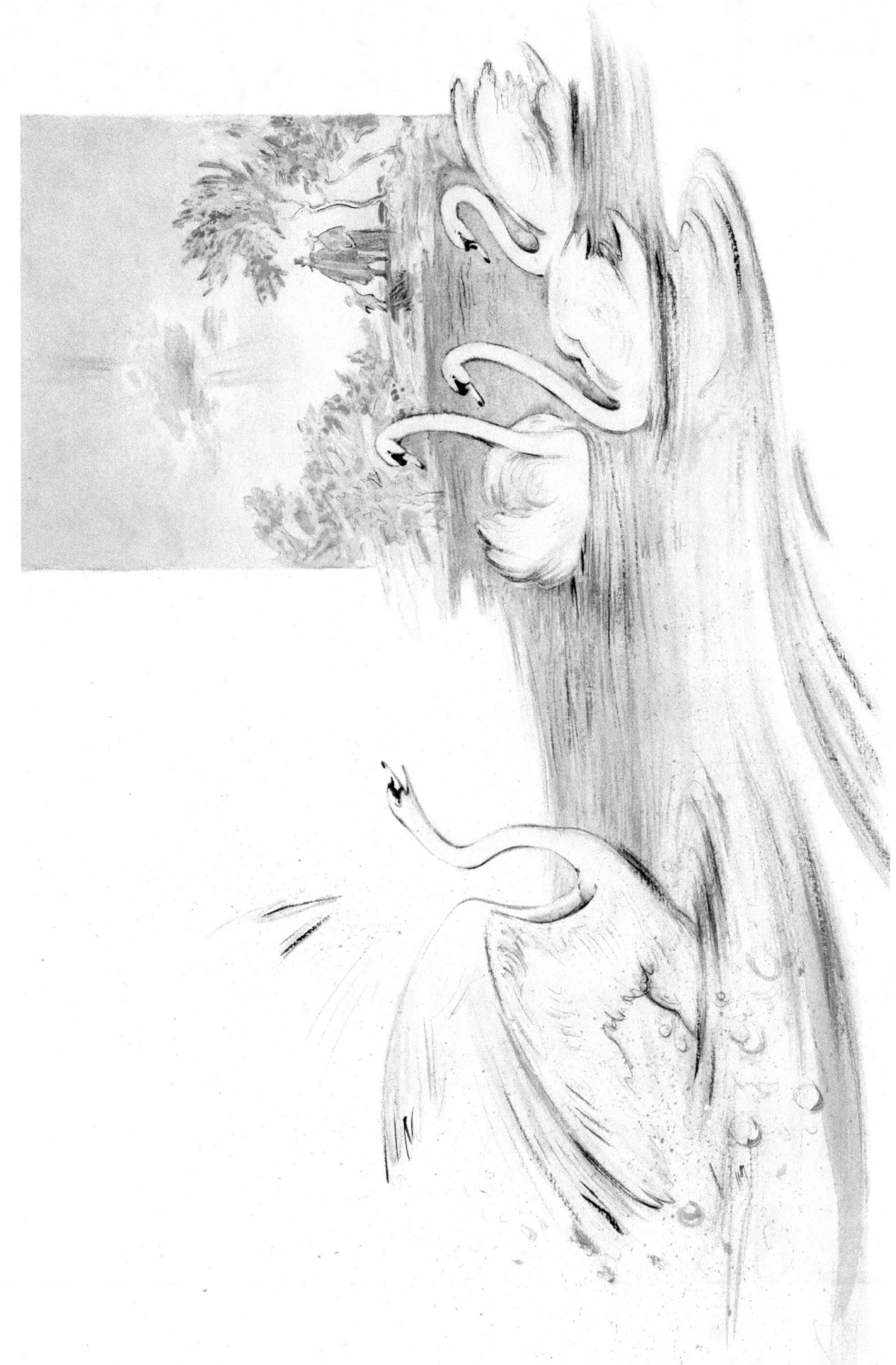

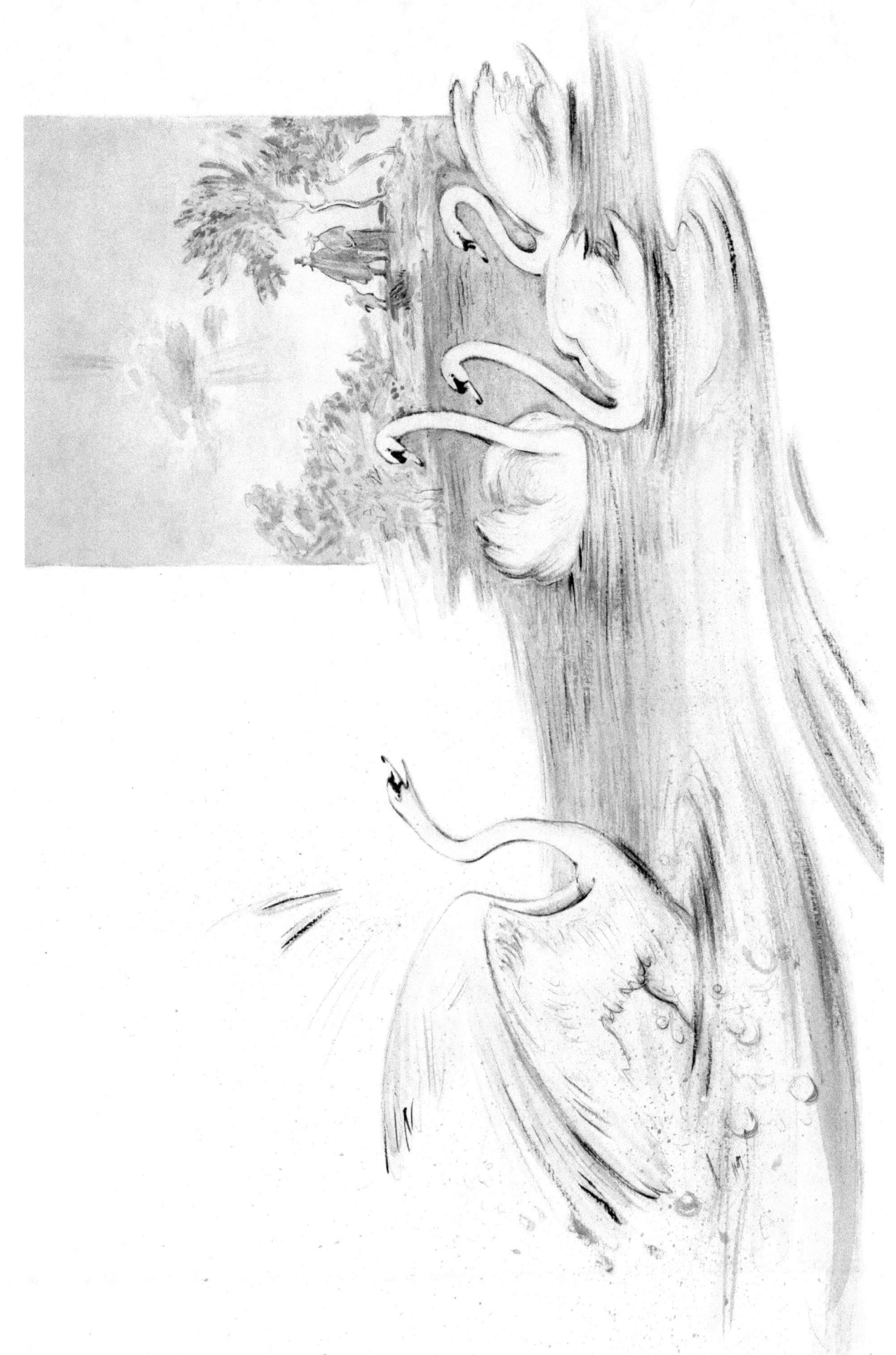

The Emperor's New Clothes

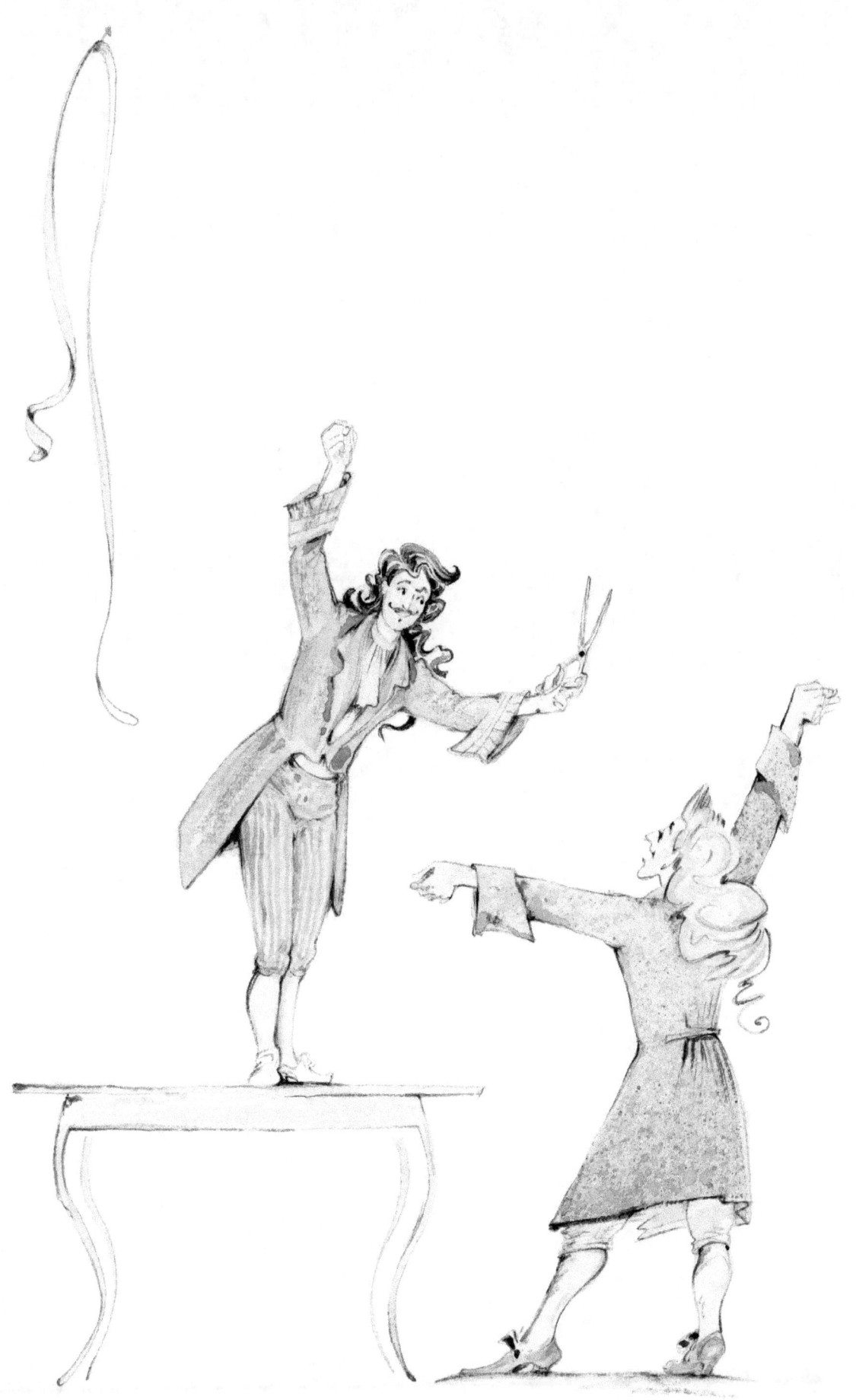

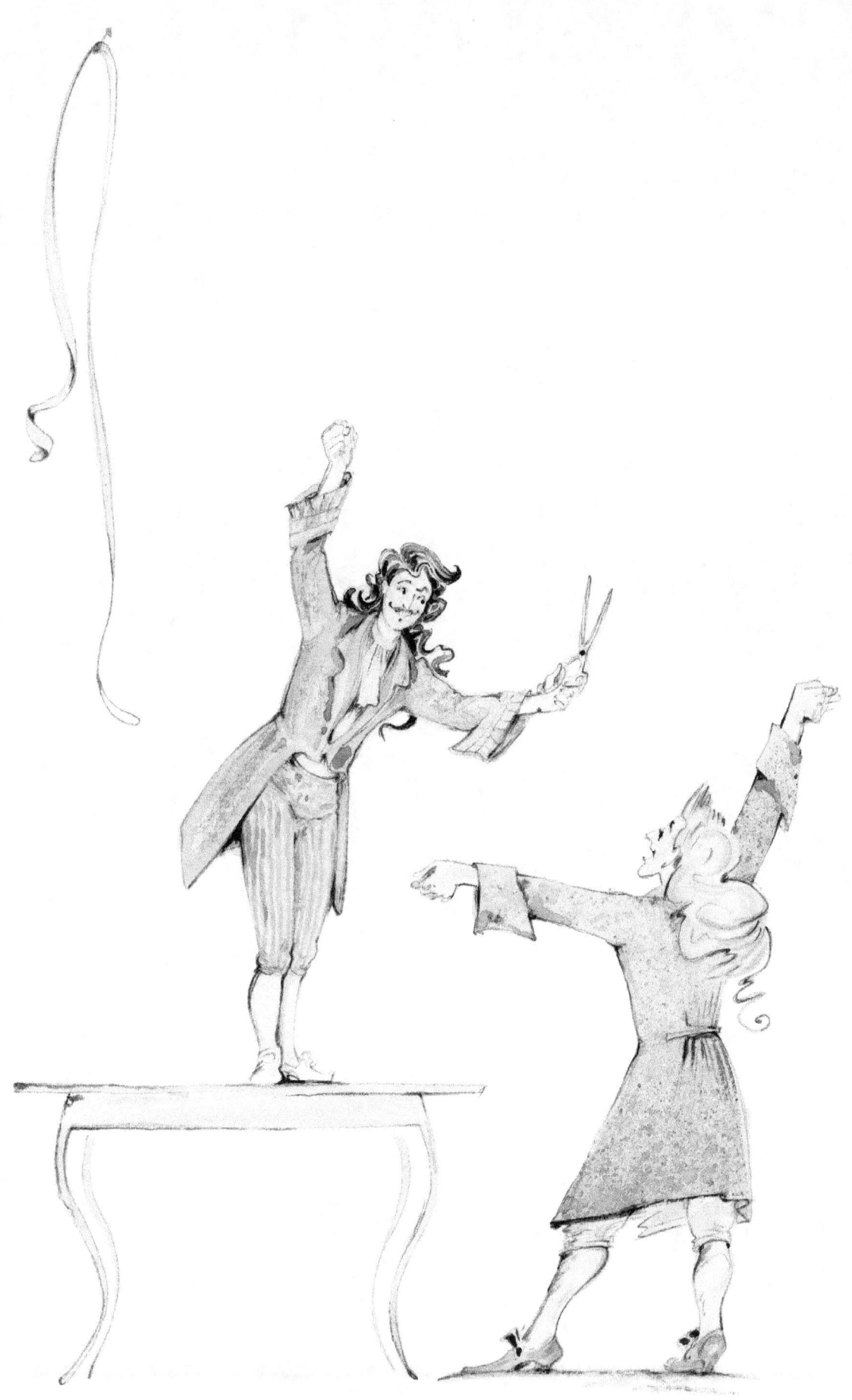

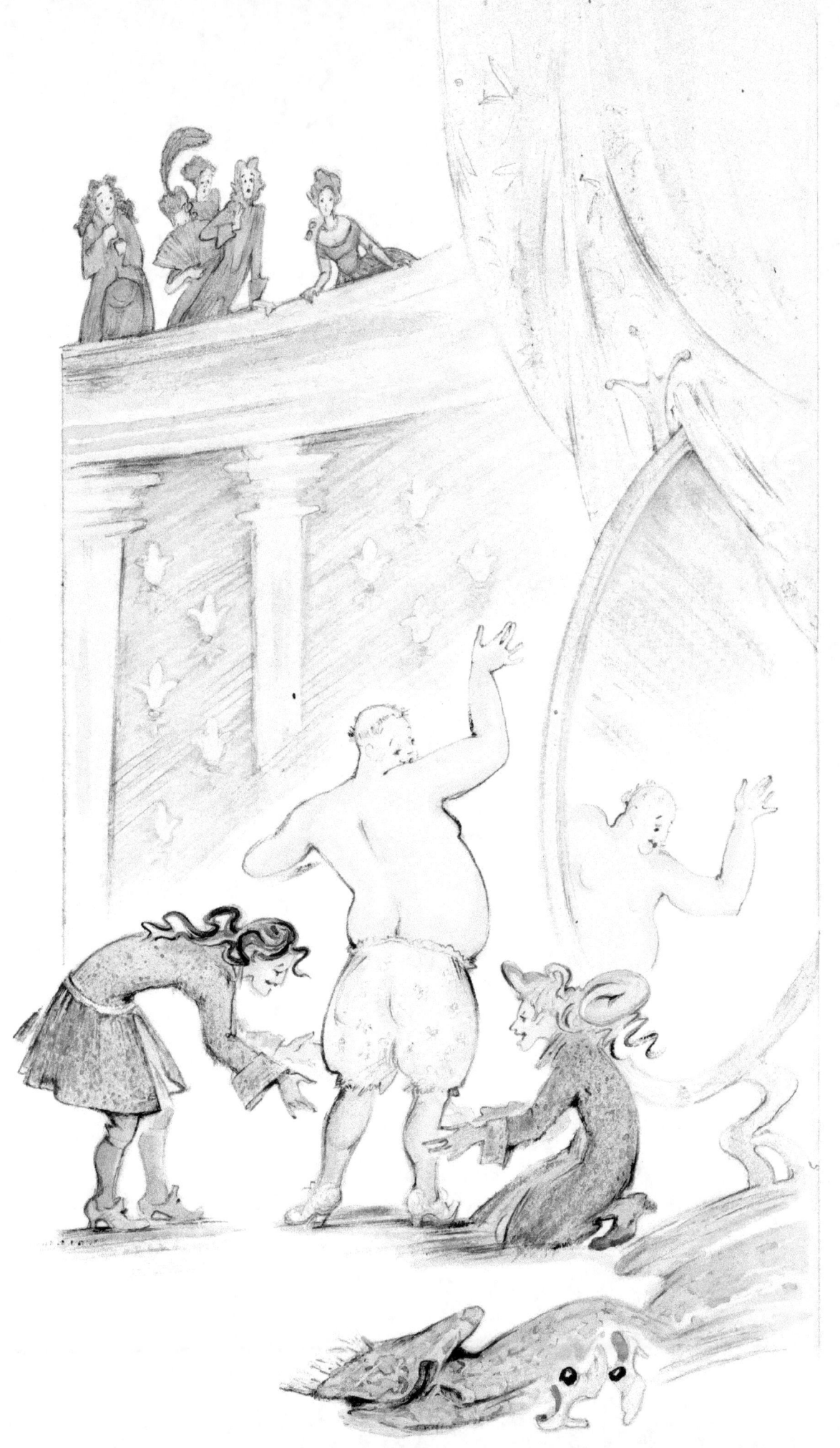

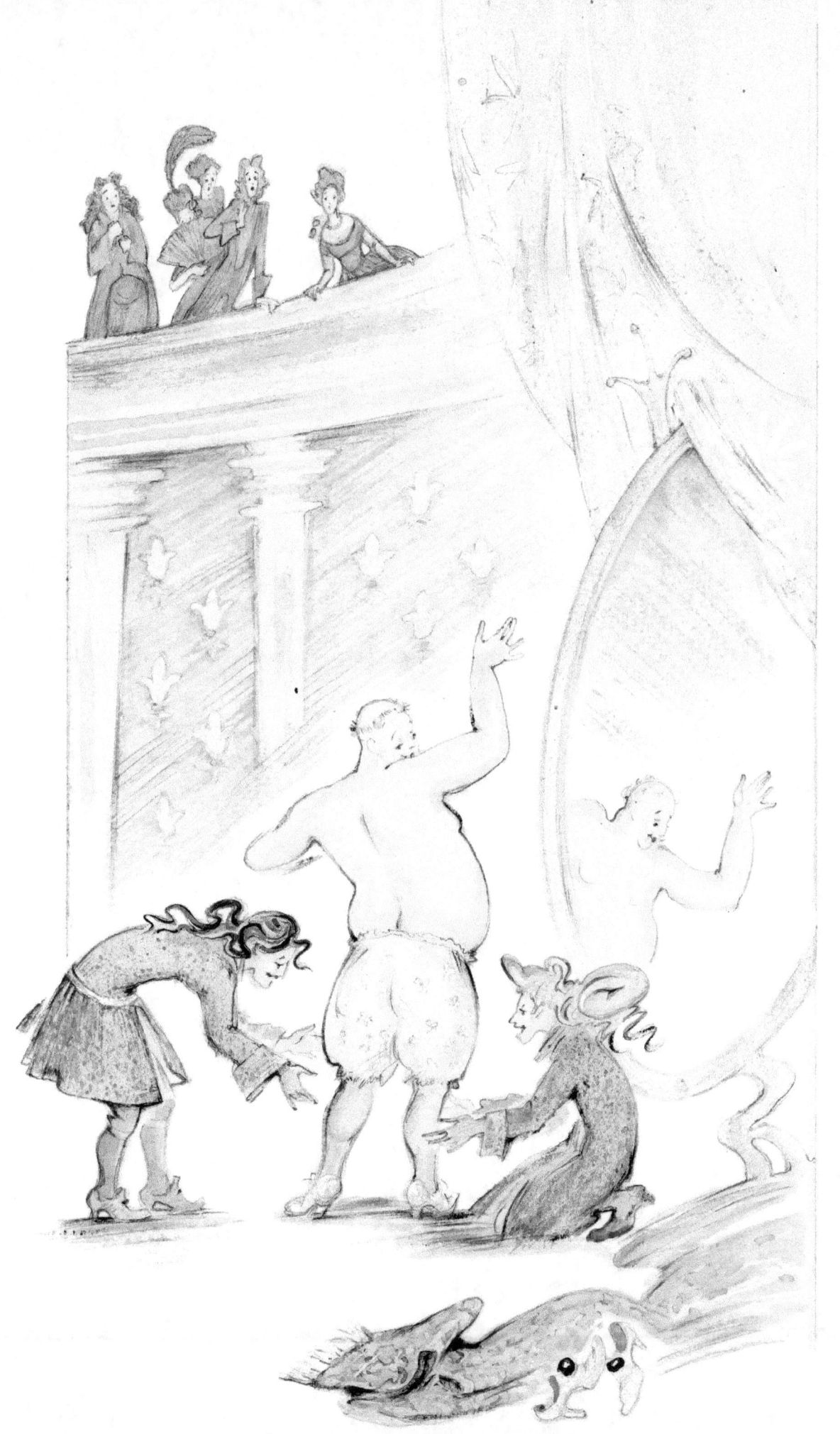

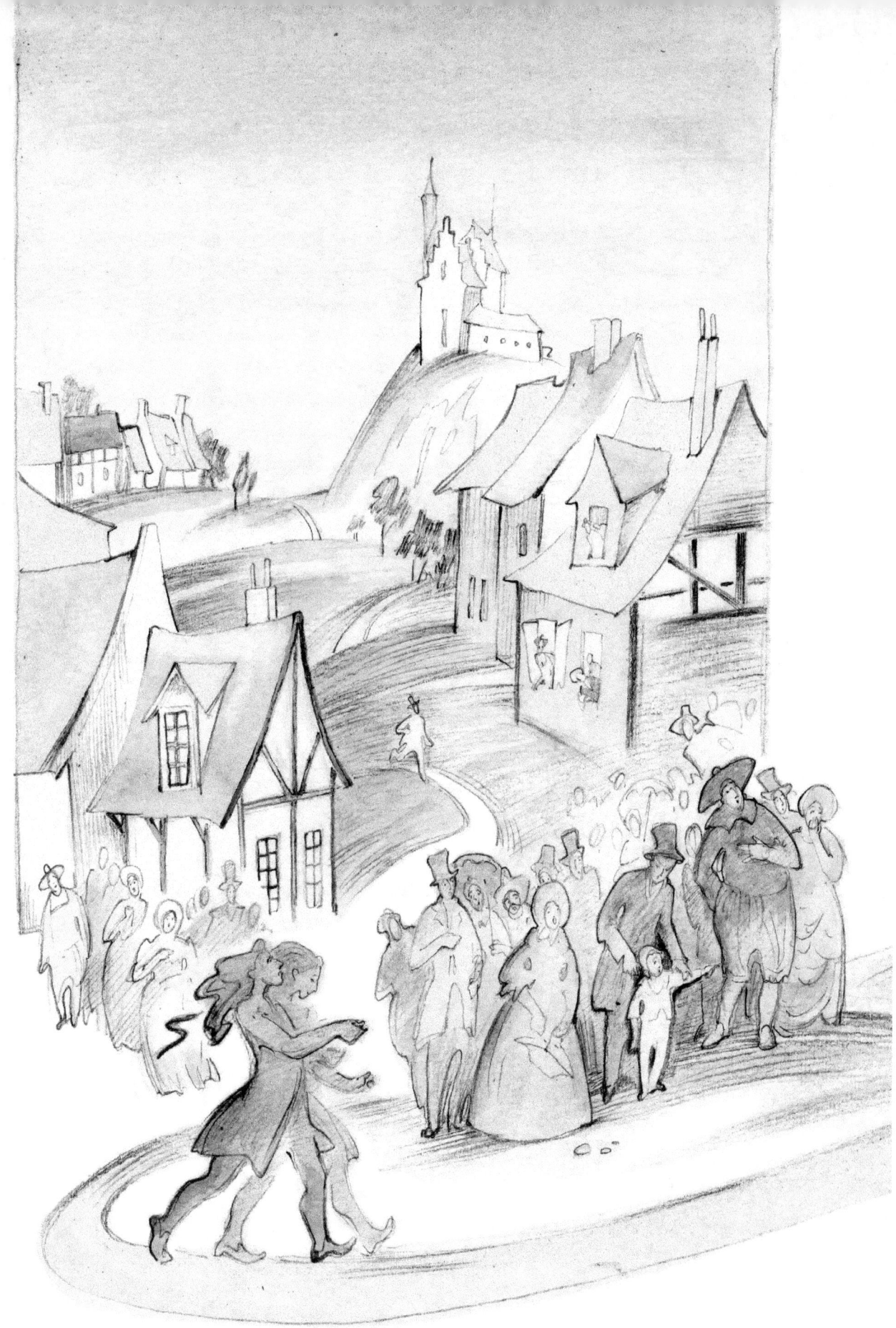

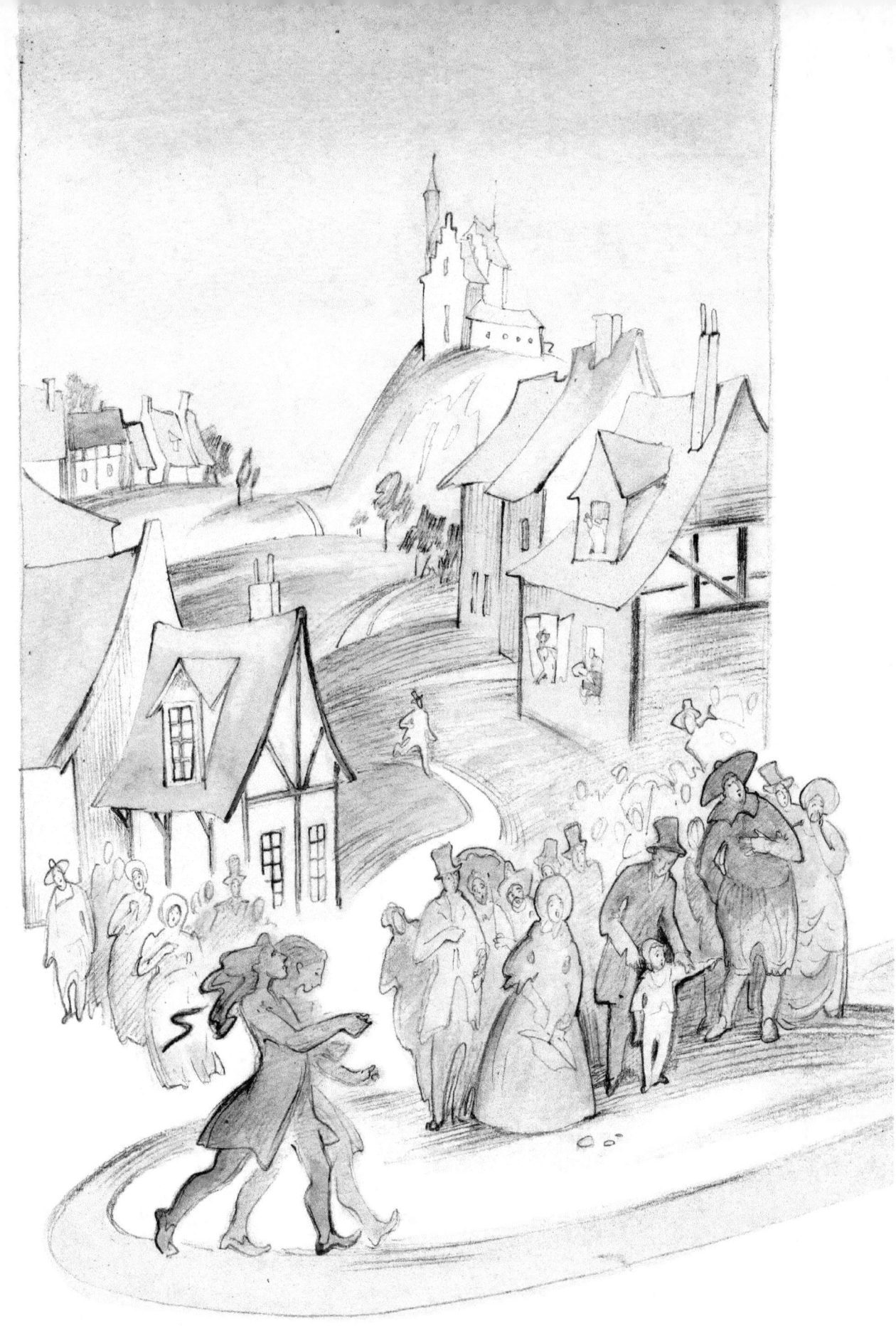

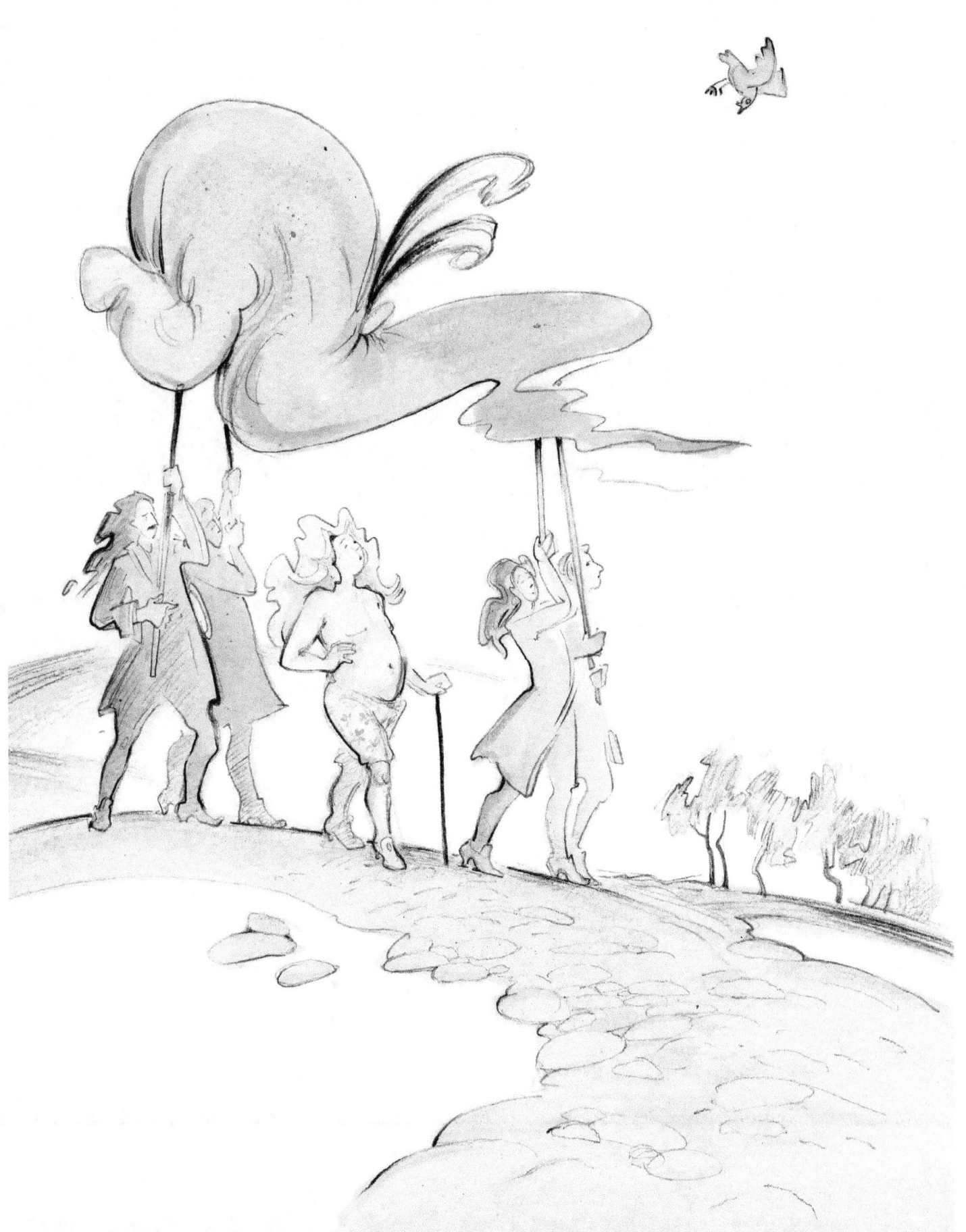

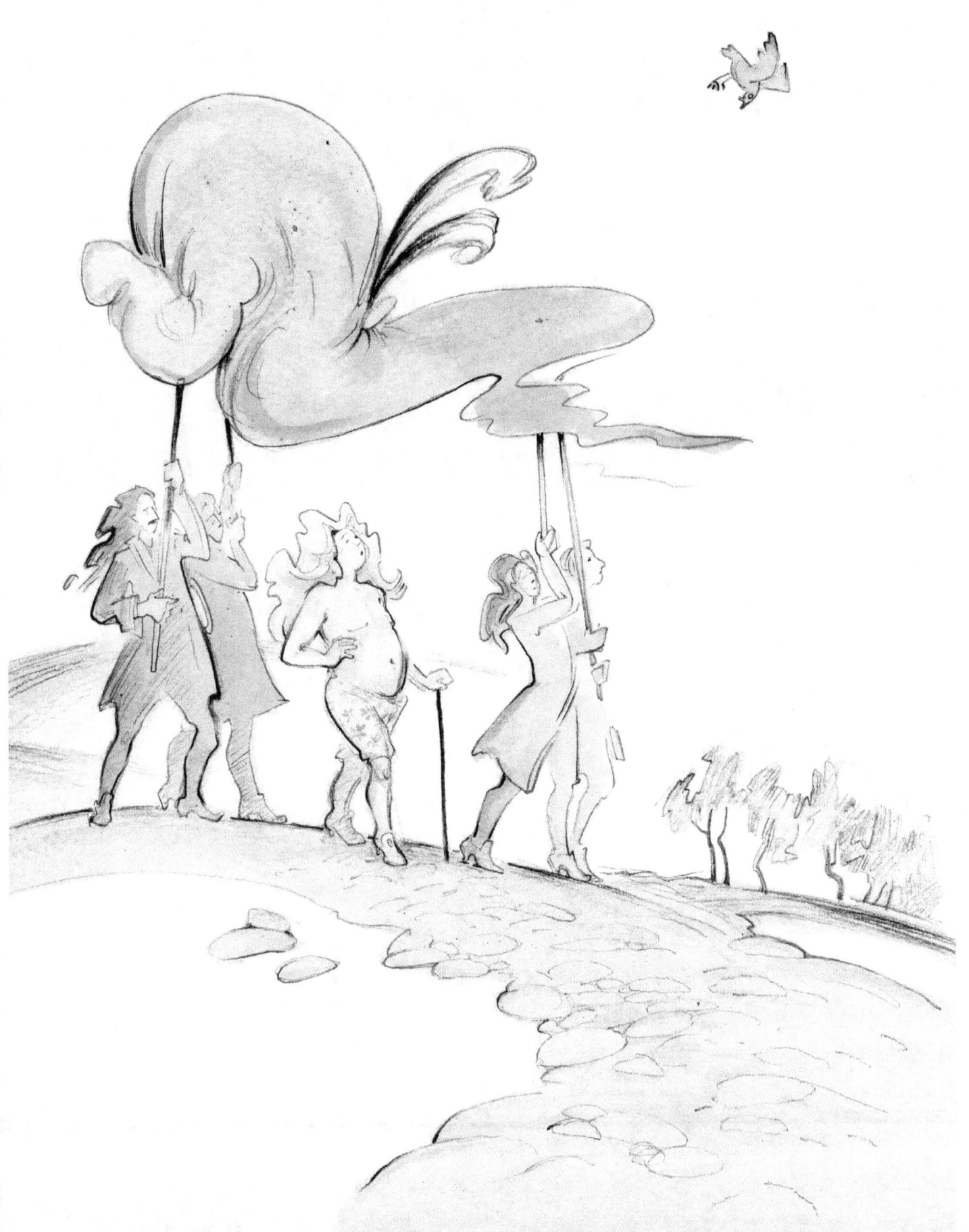

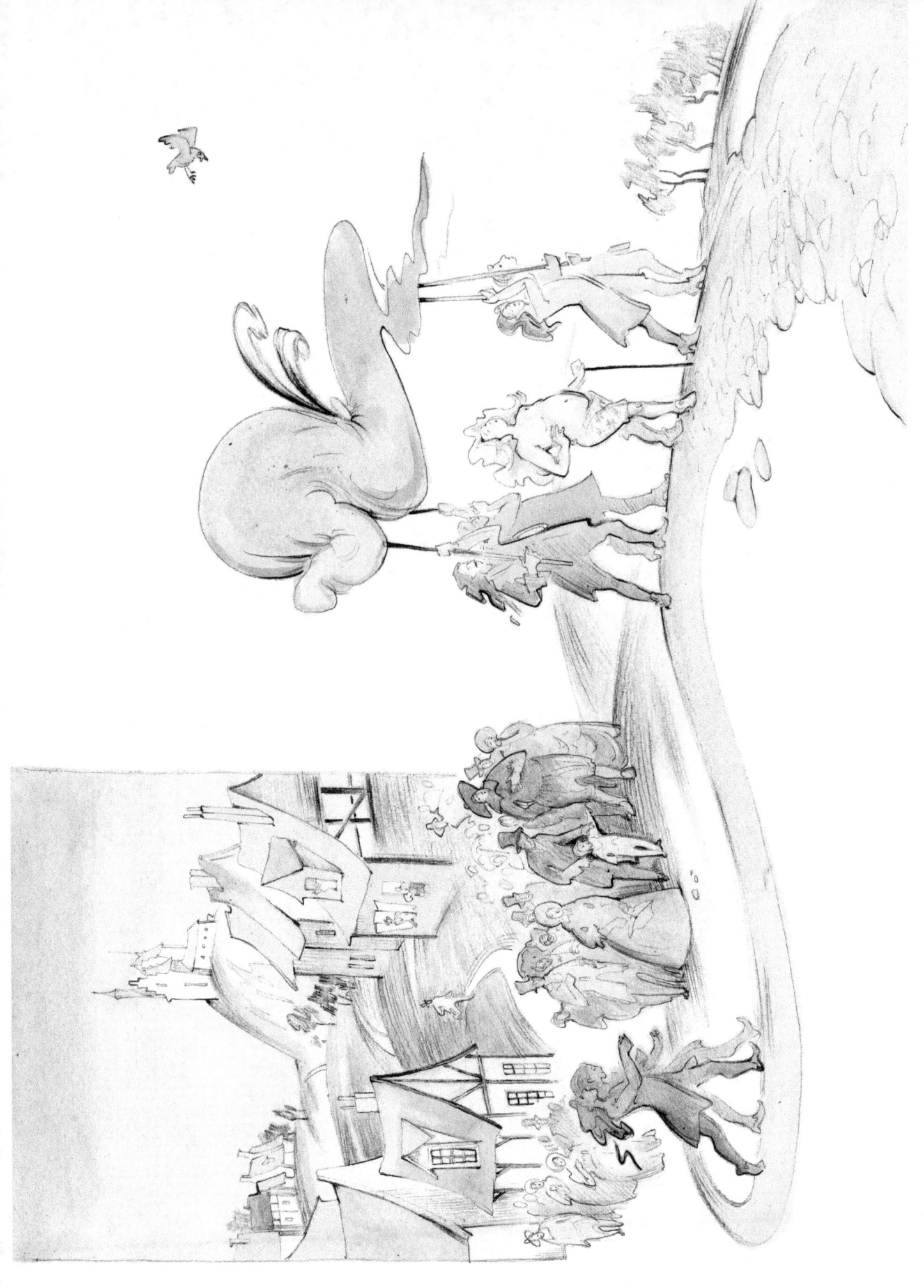

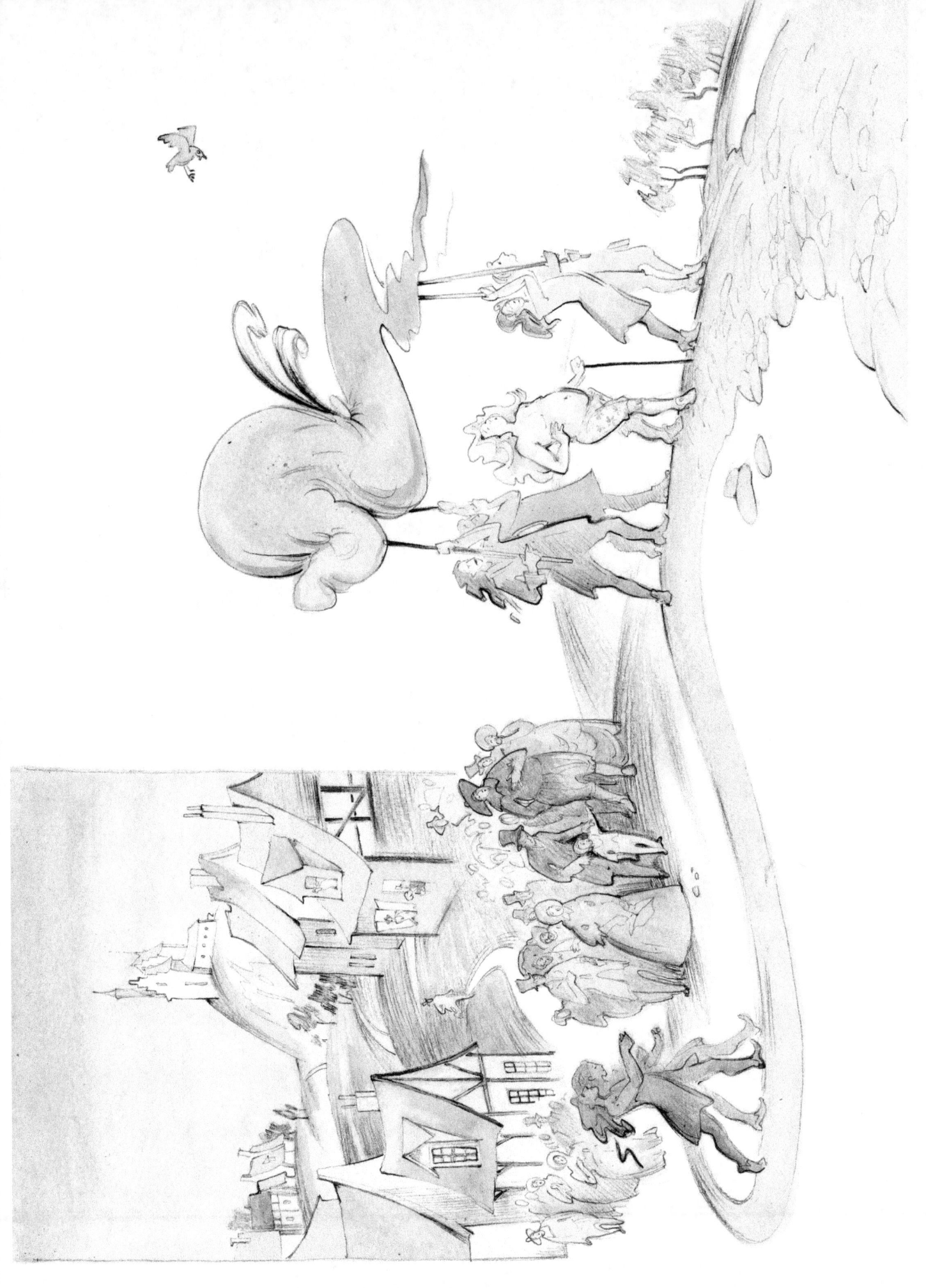

The Swineherd

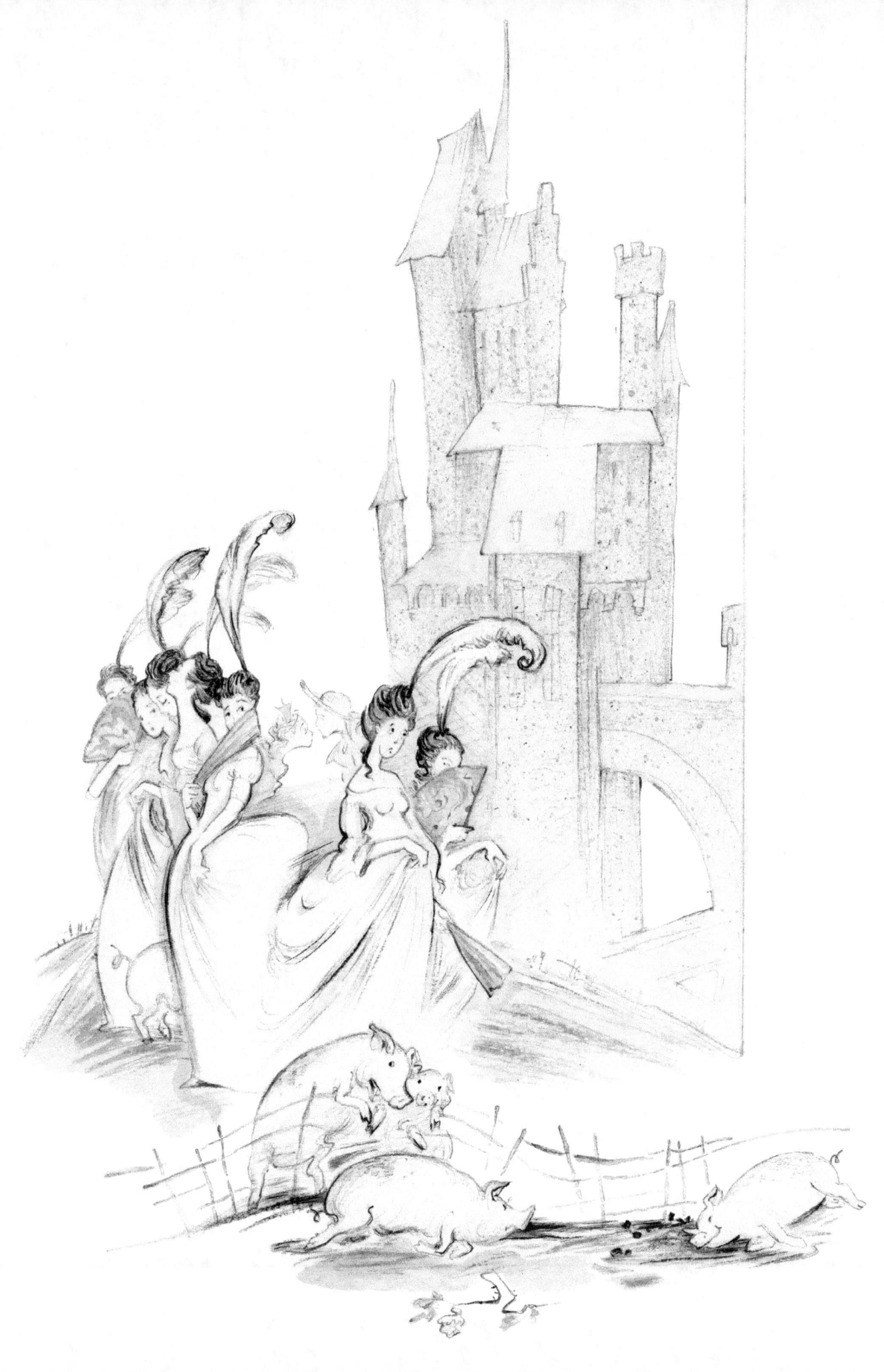

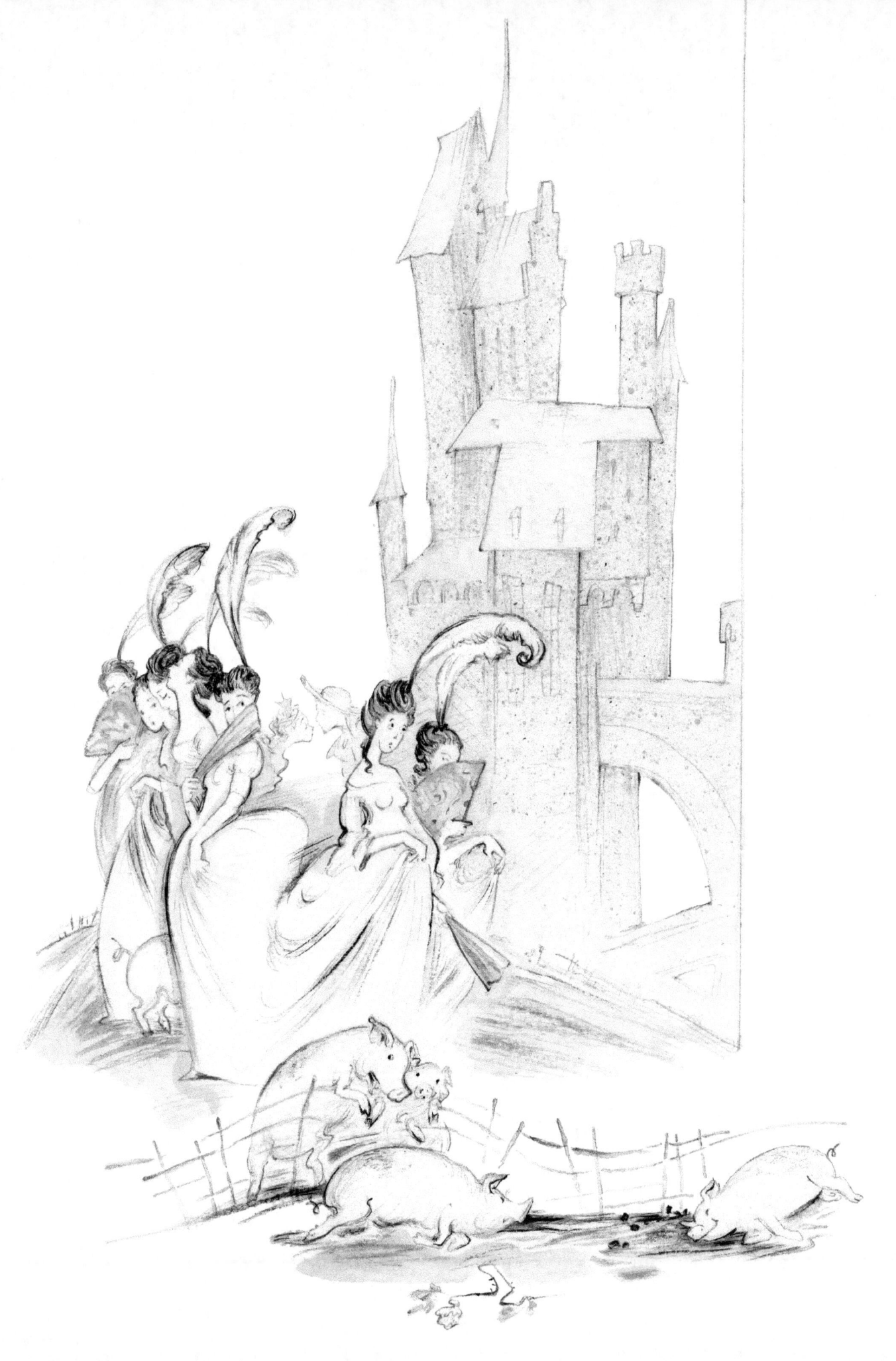

The Nightingale

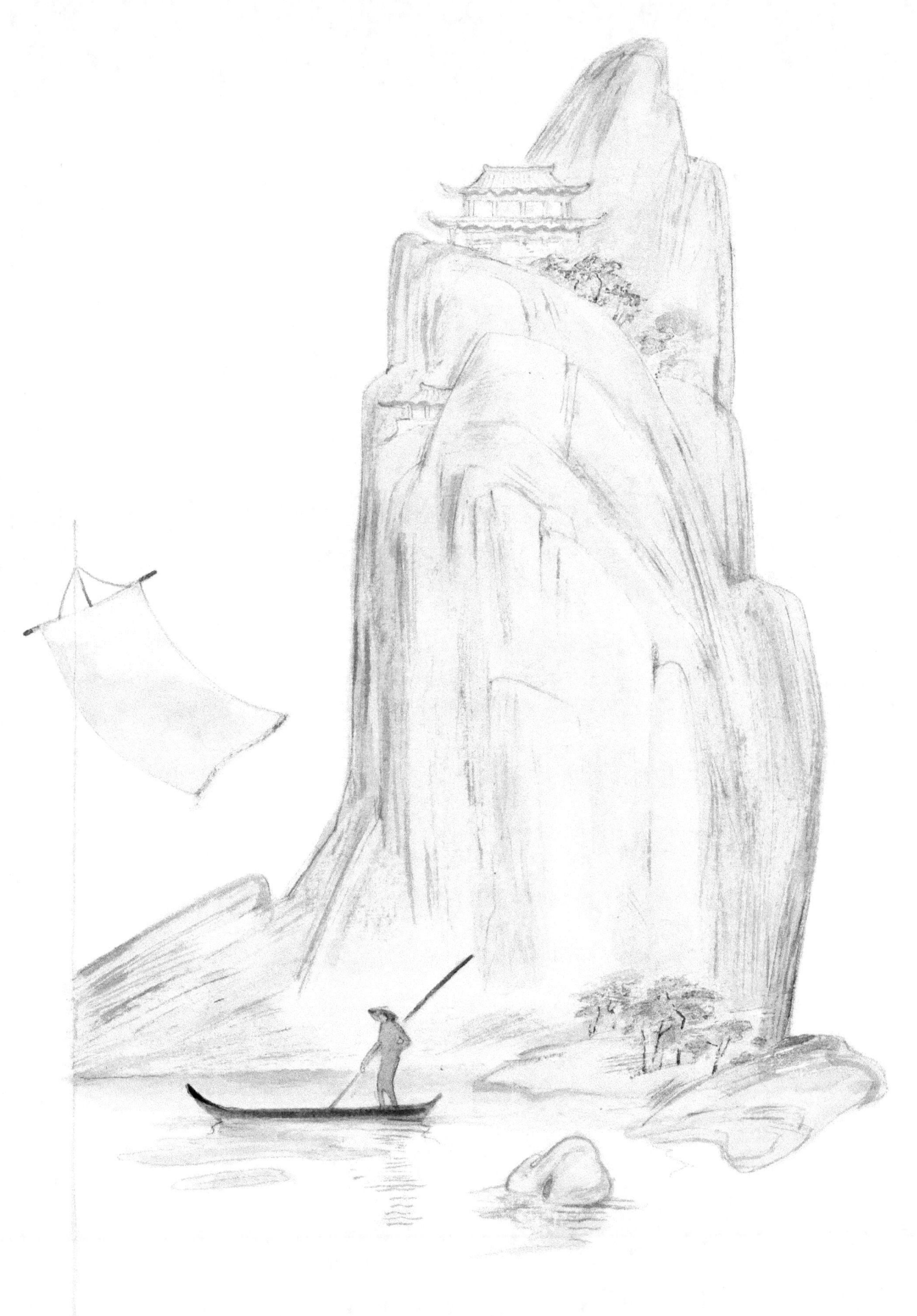

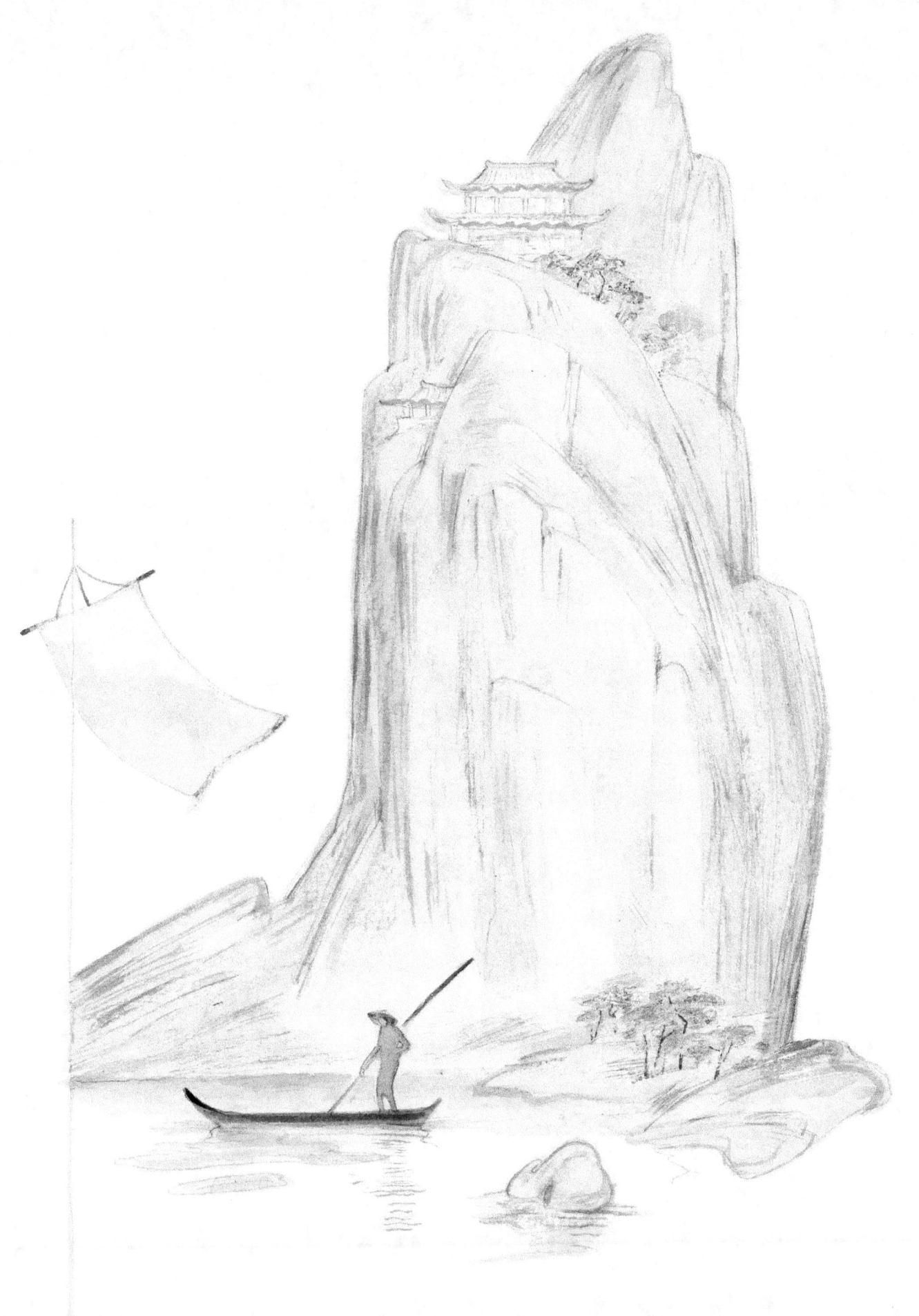

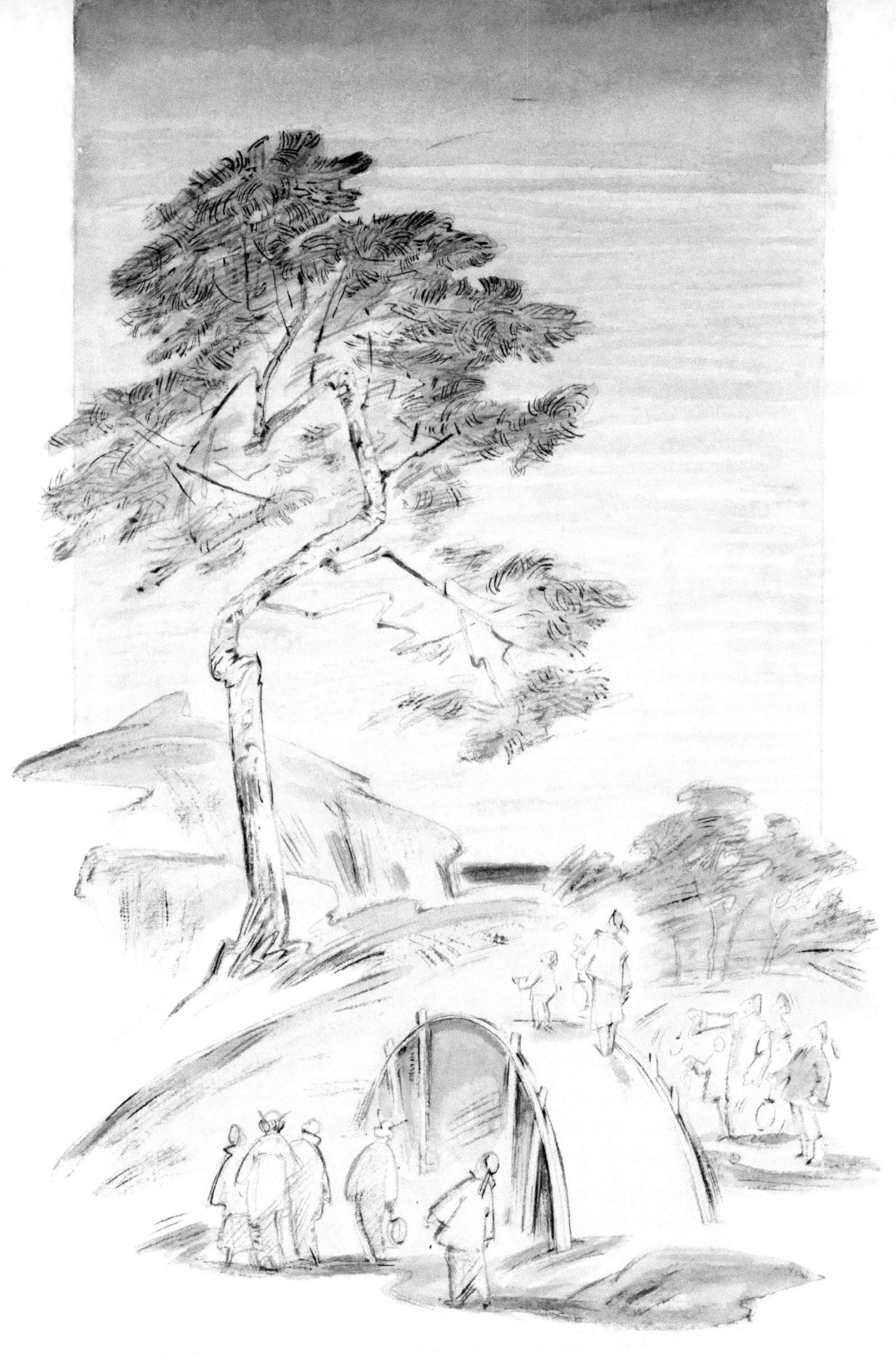

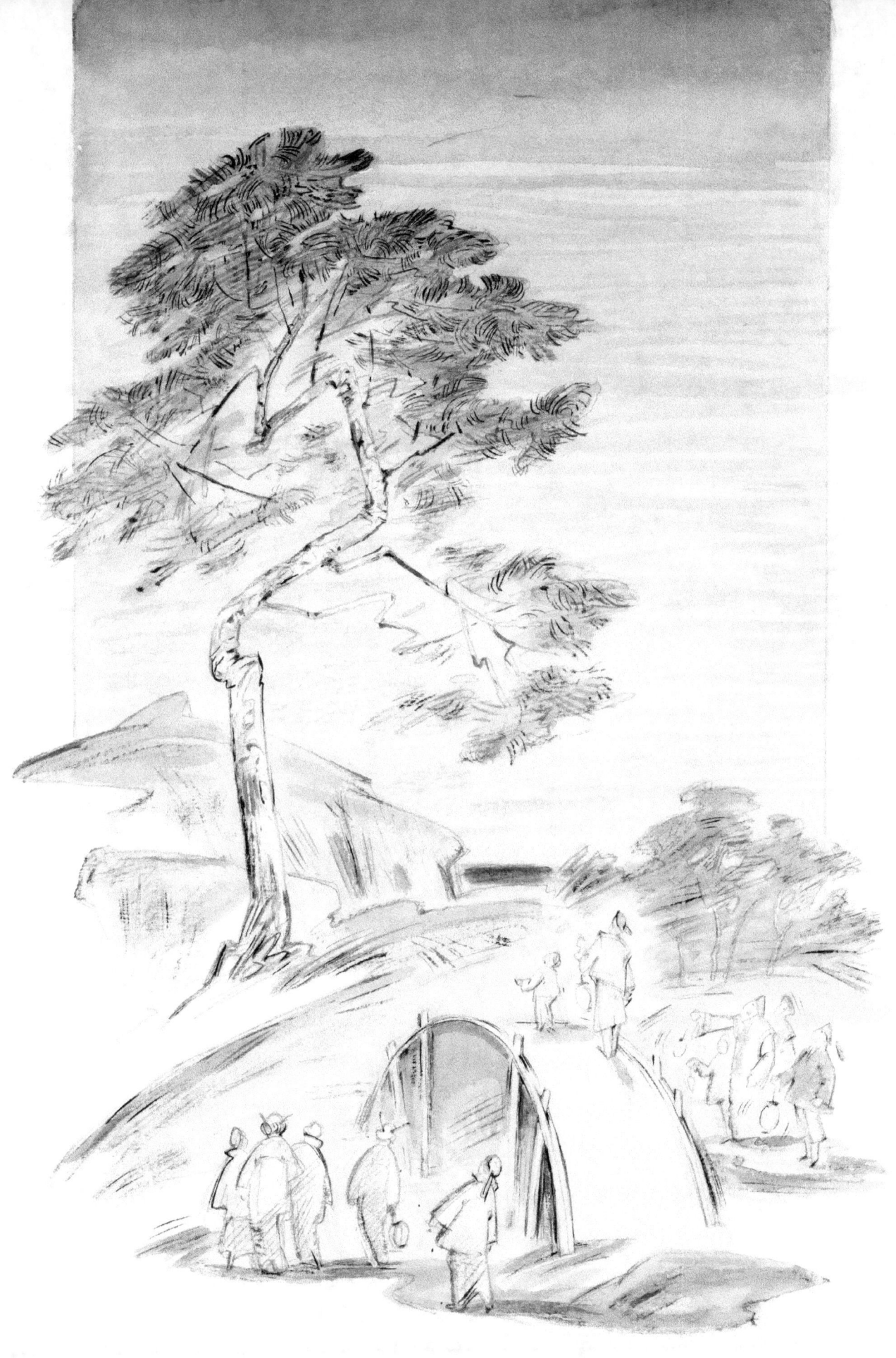

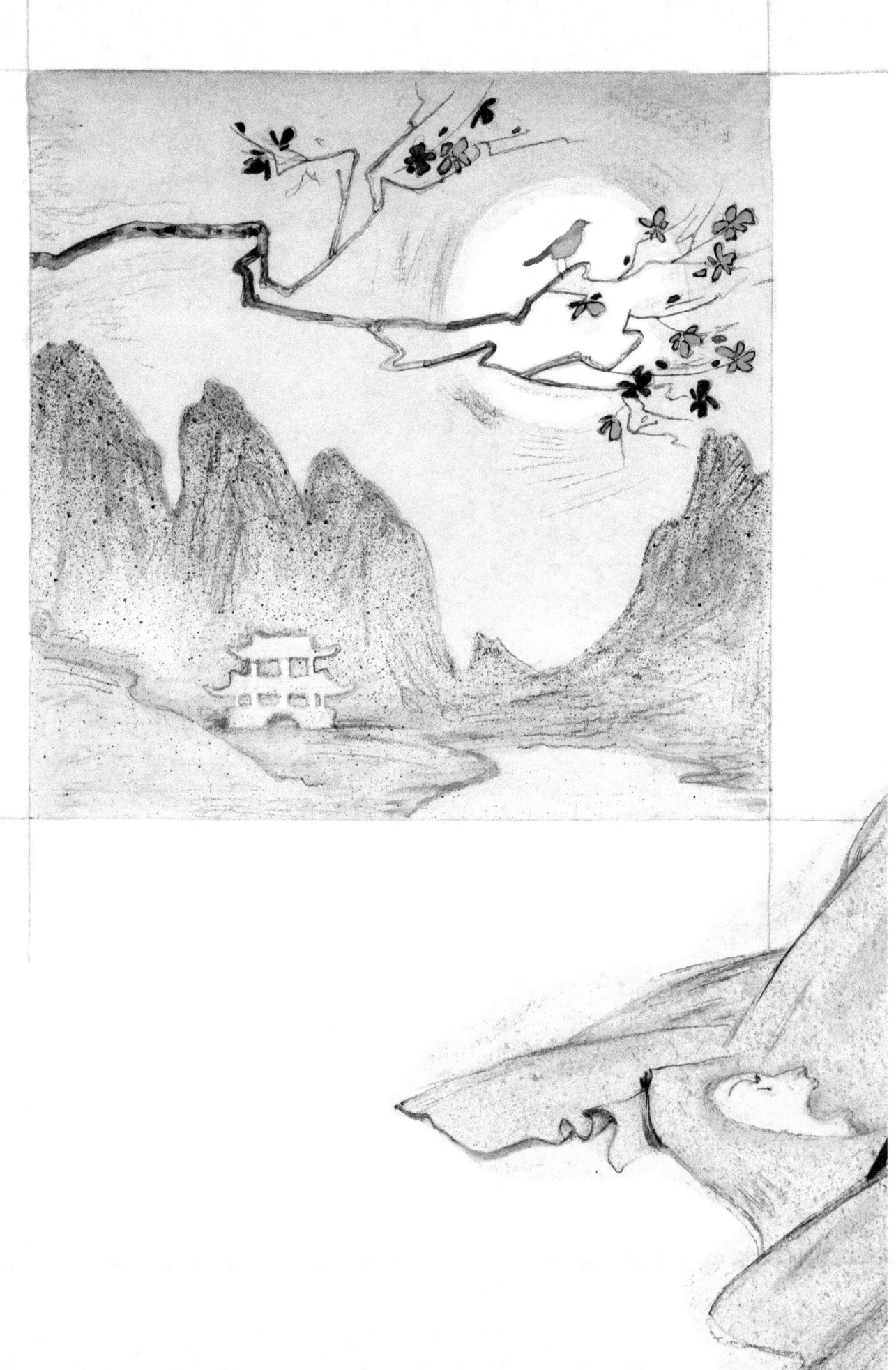

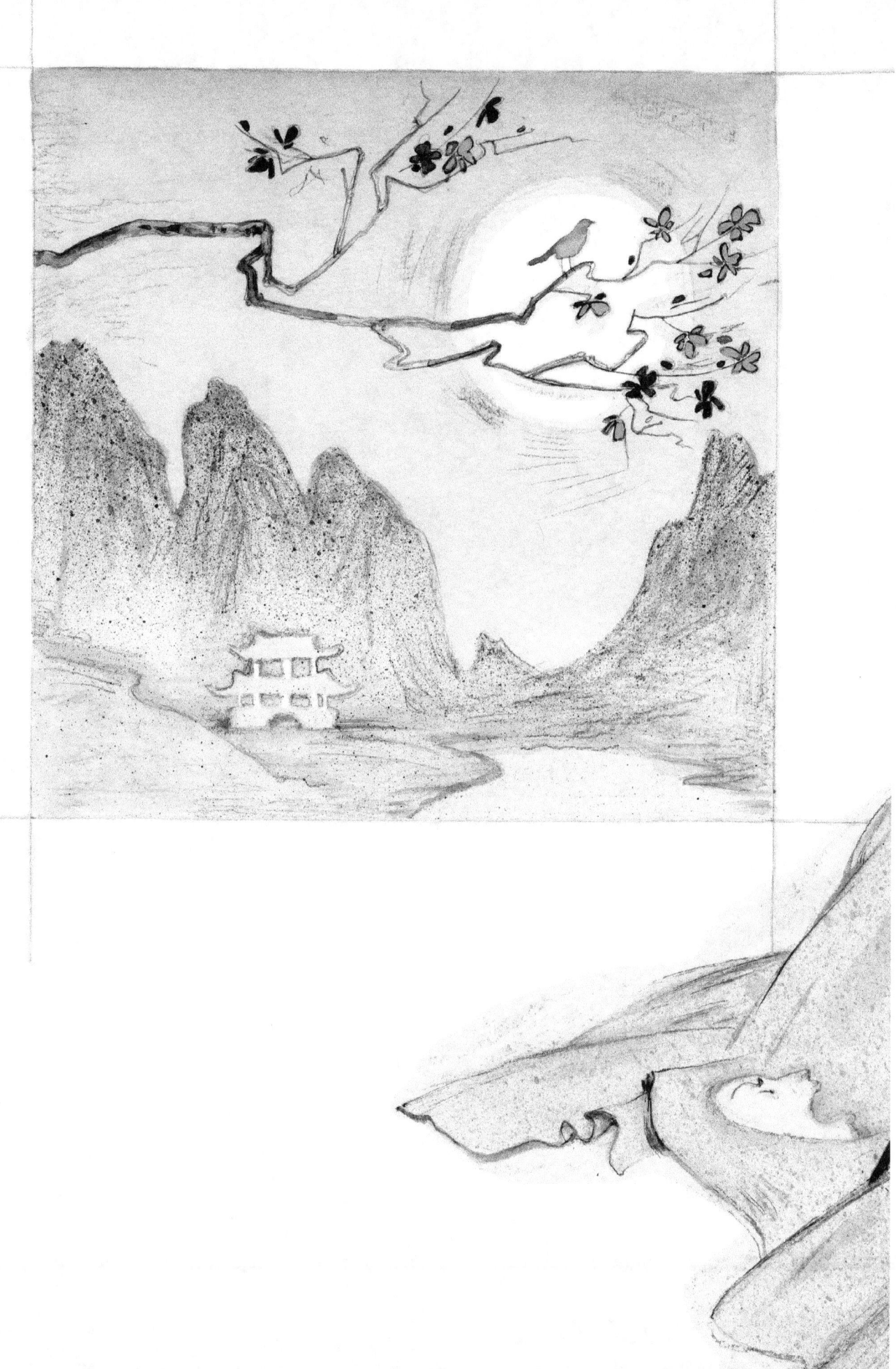

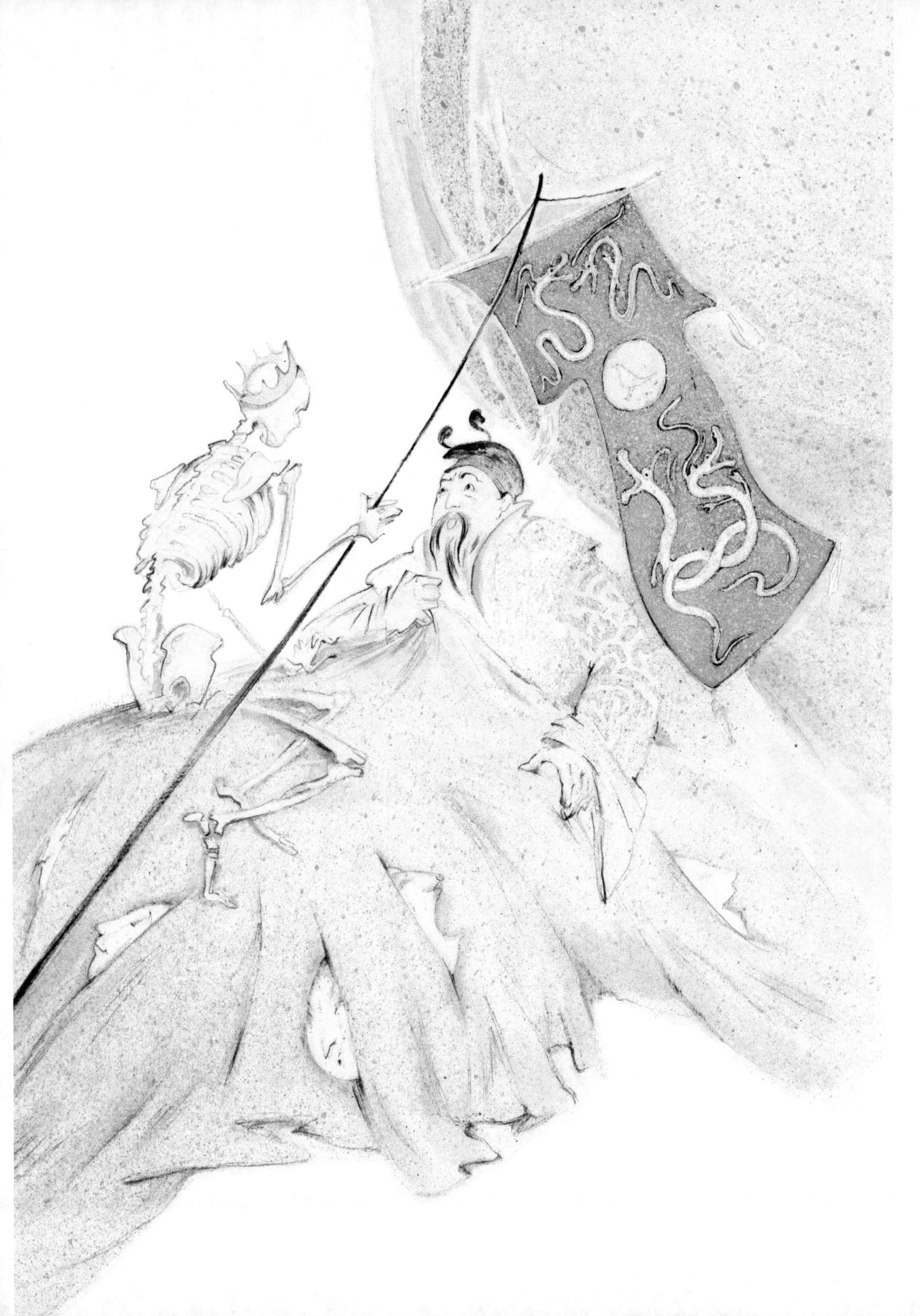

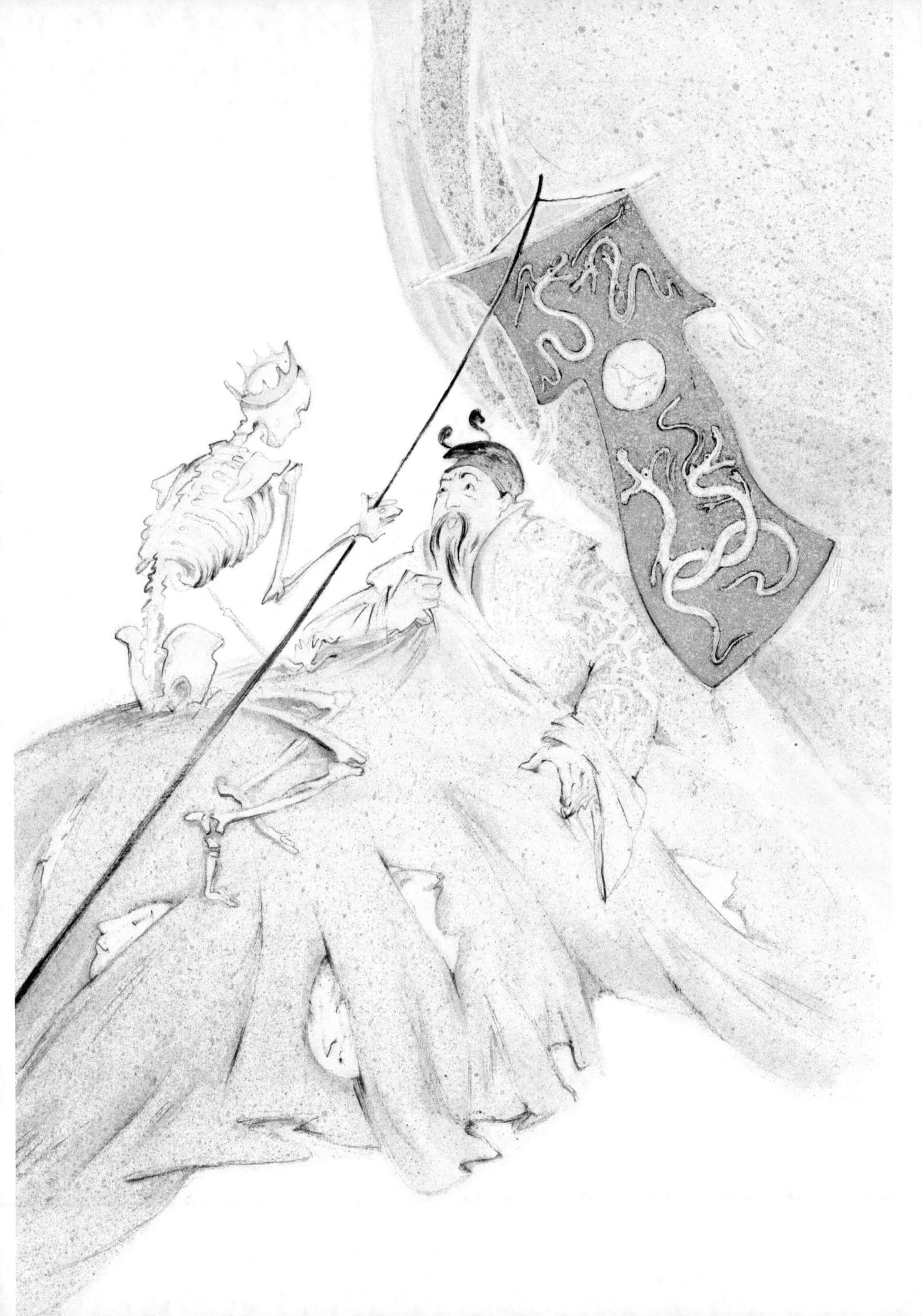

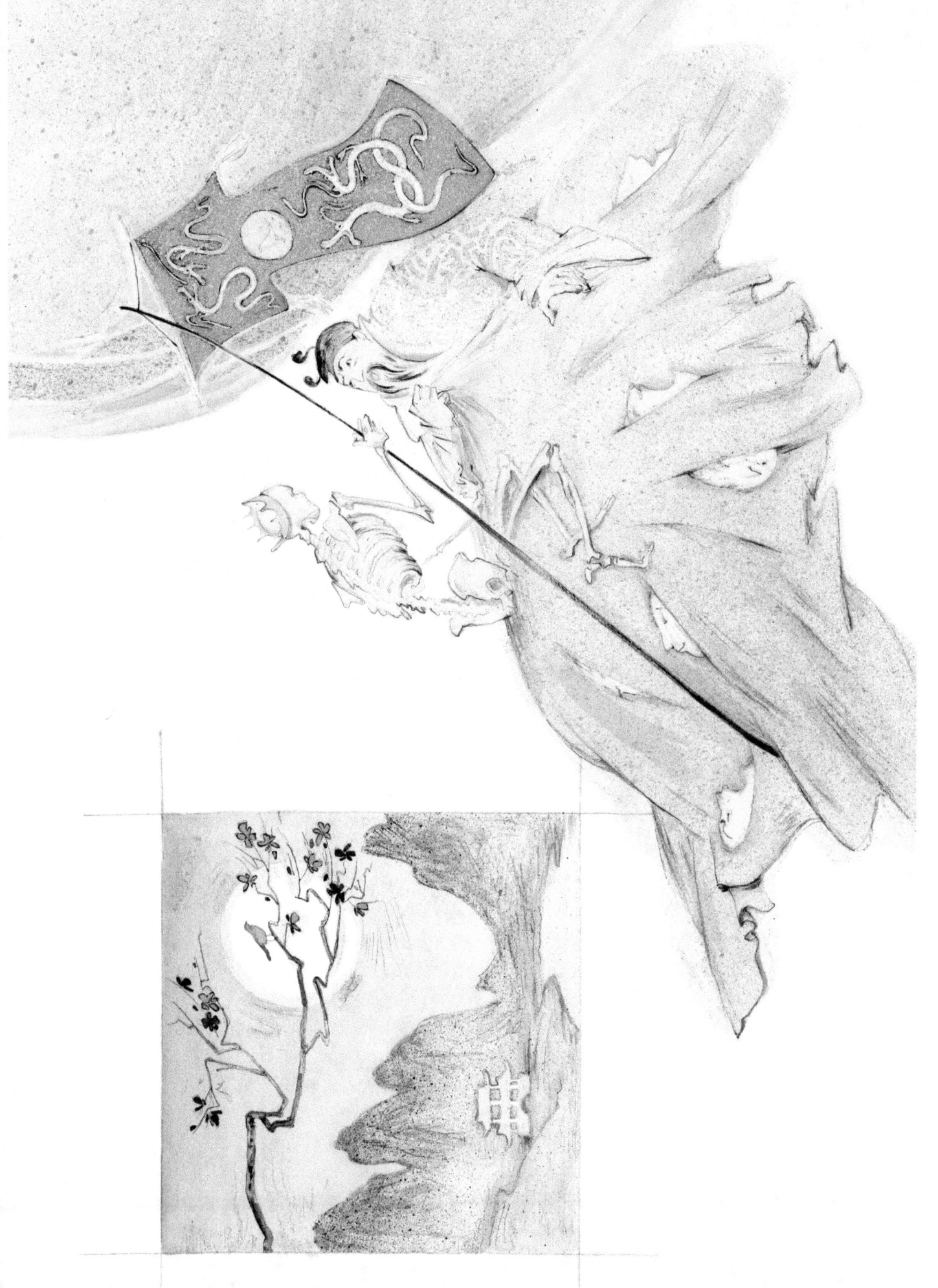

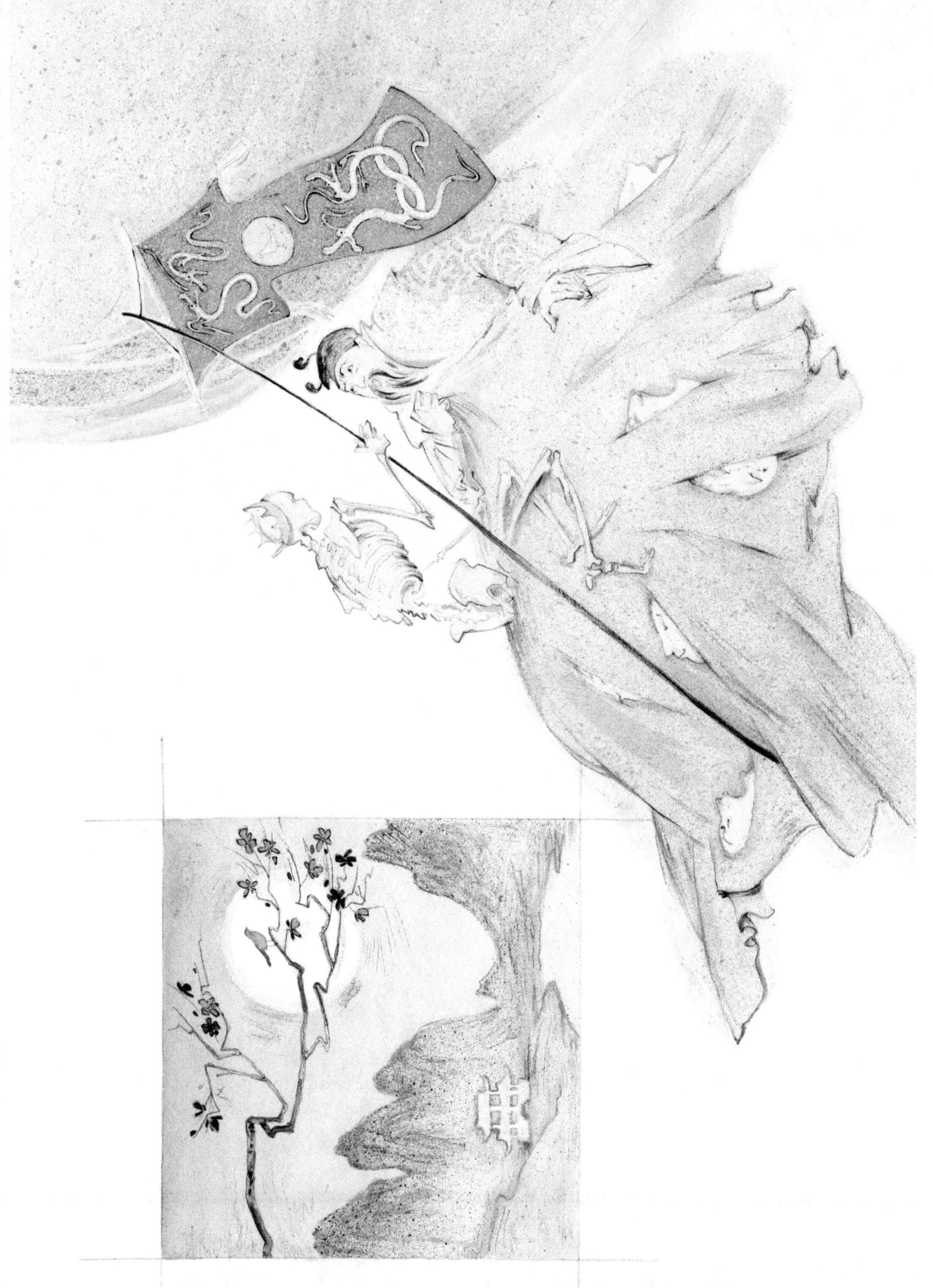

The Steadfast Tin Soldier

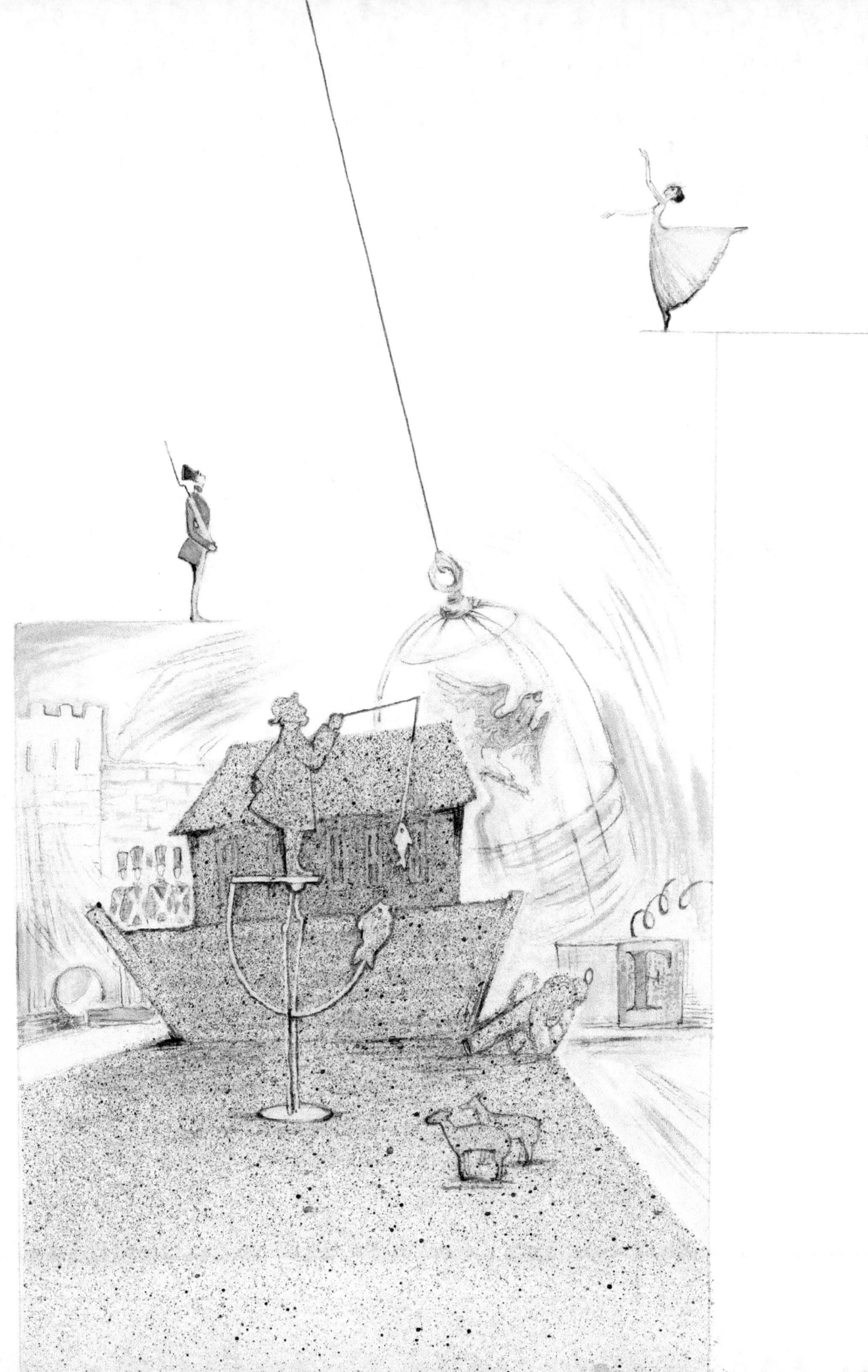

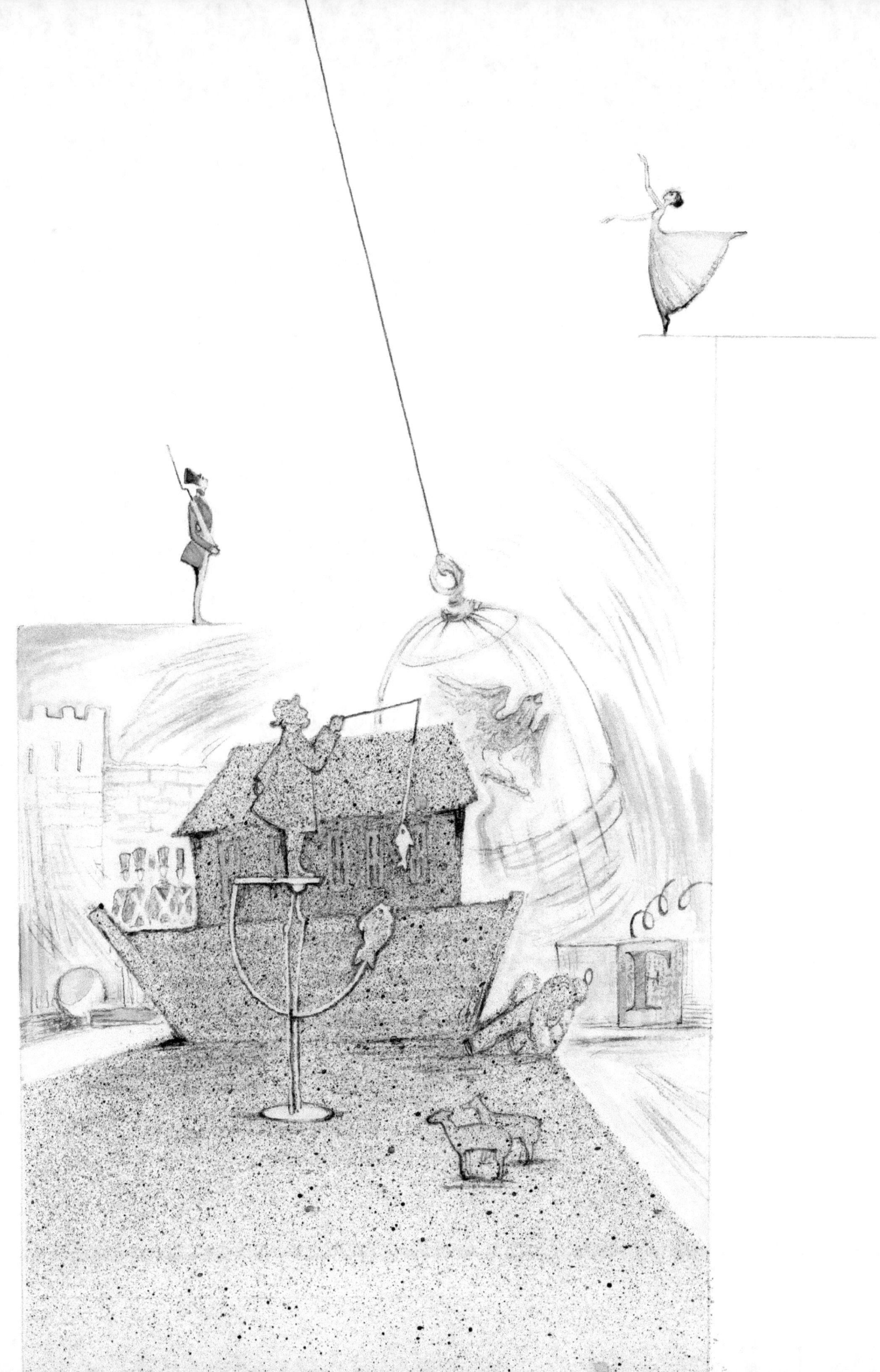

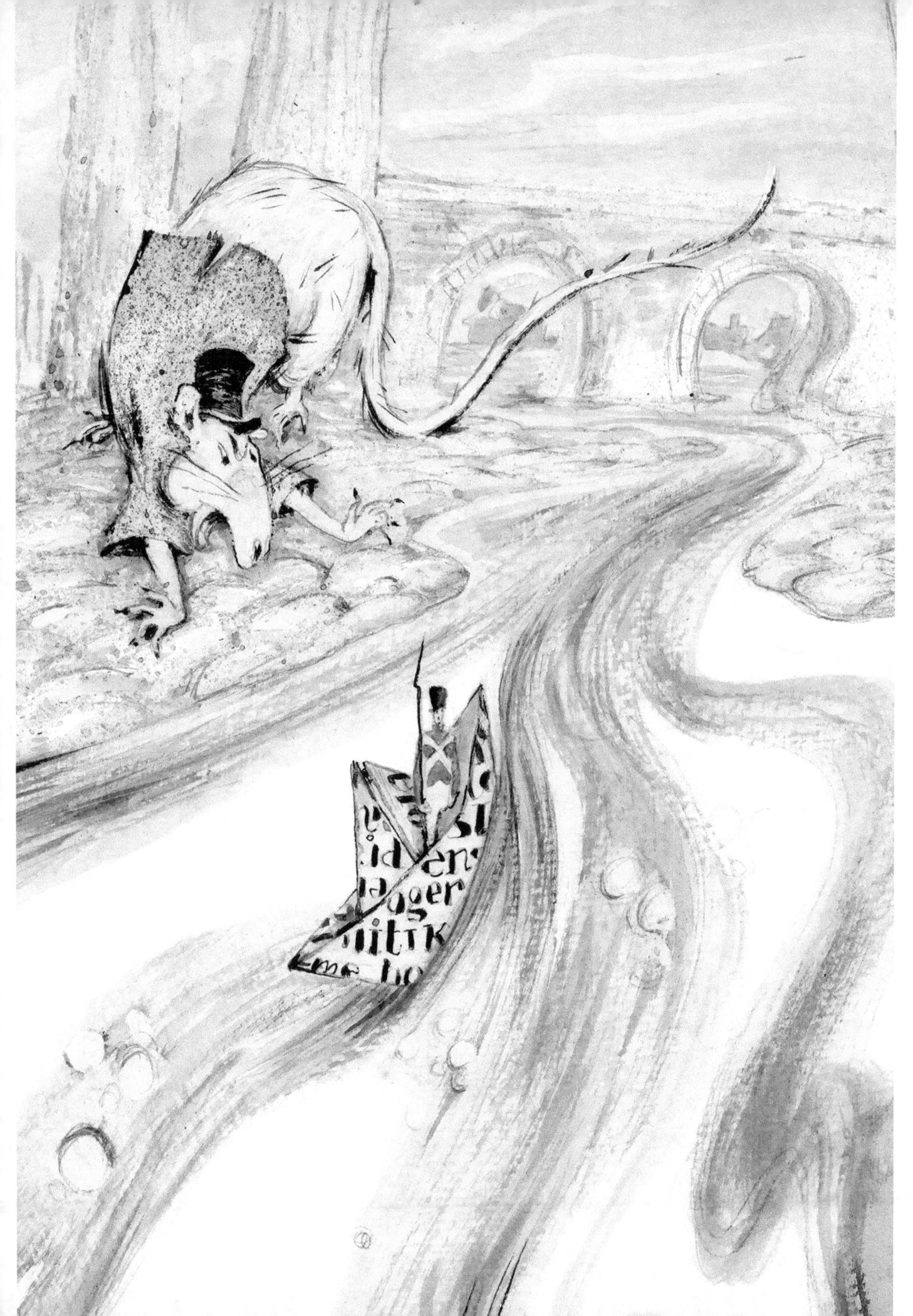

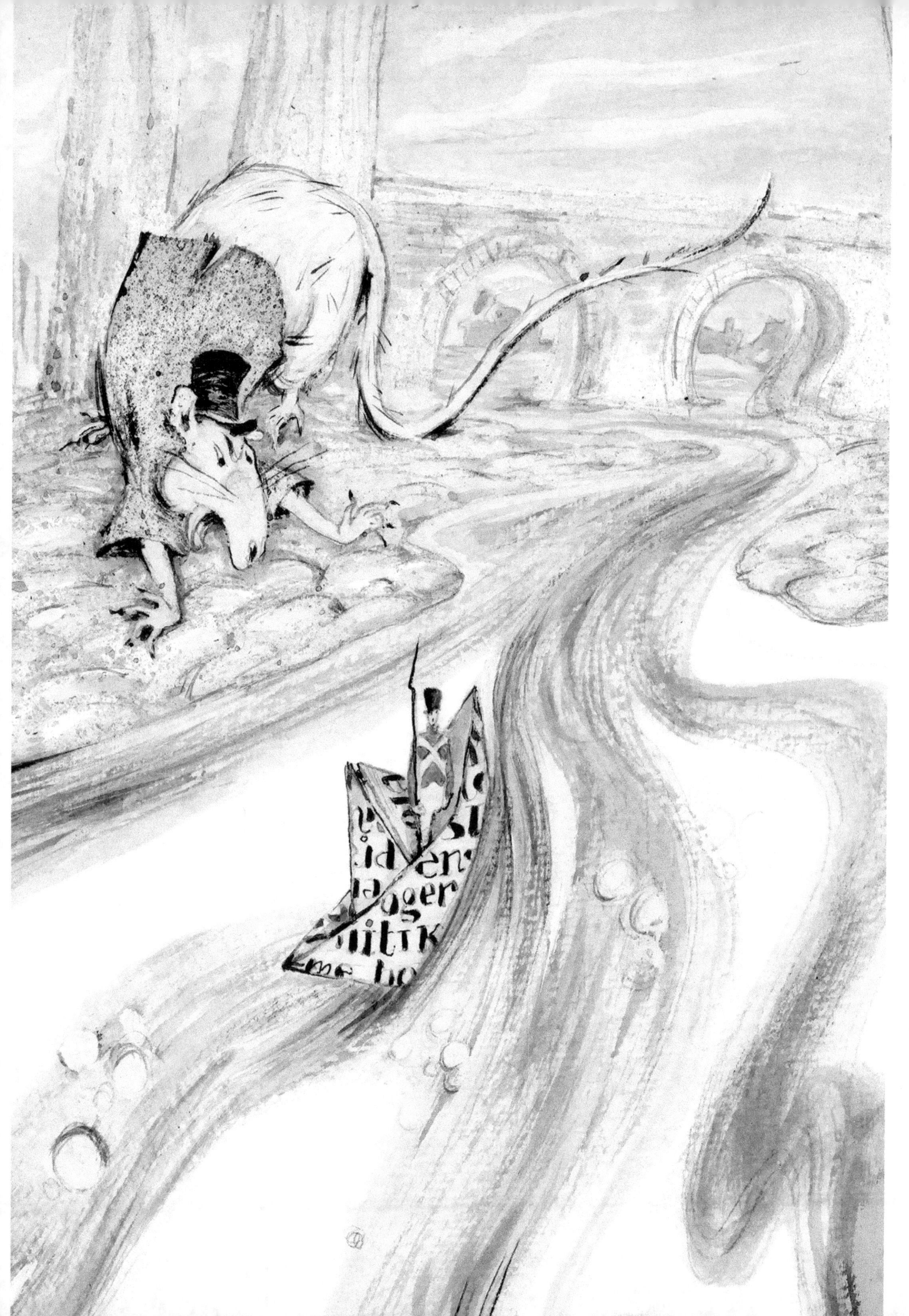

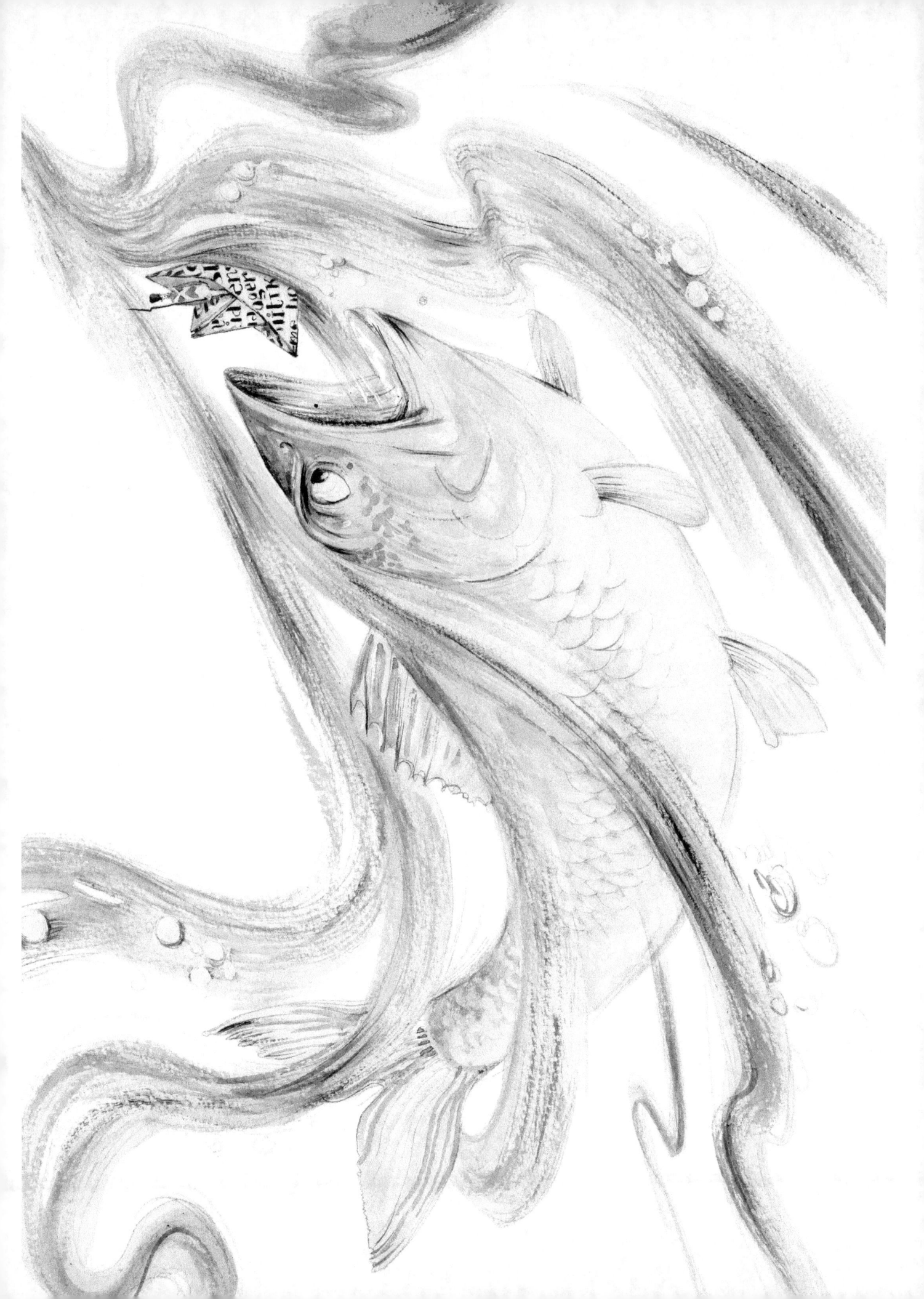

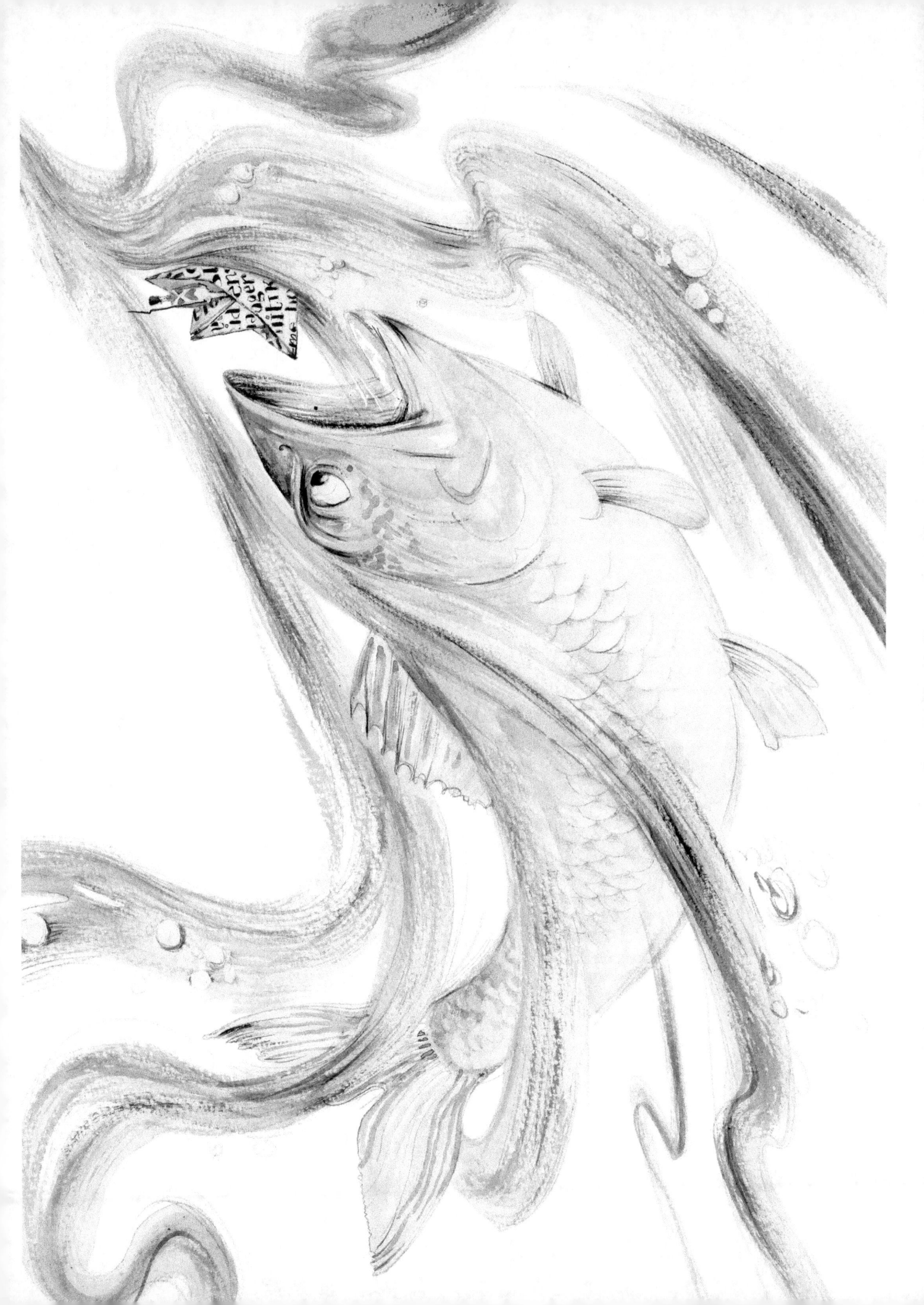

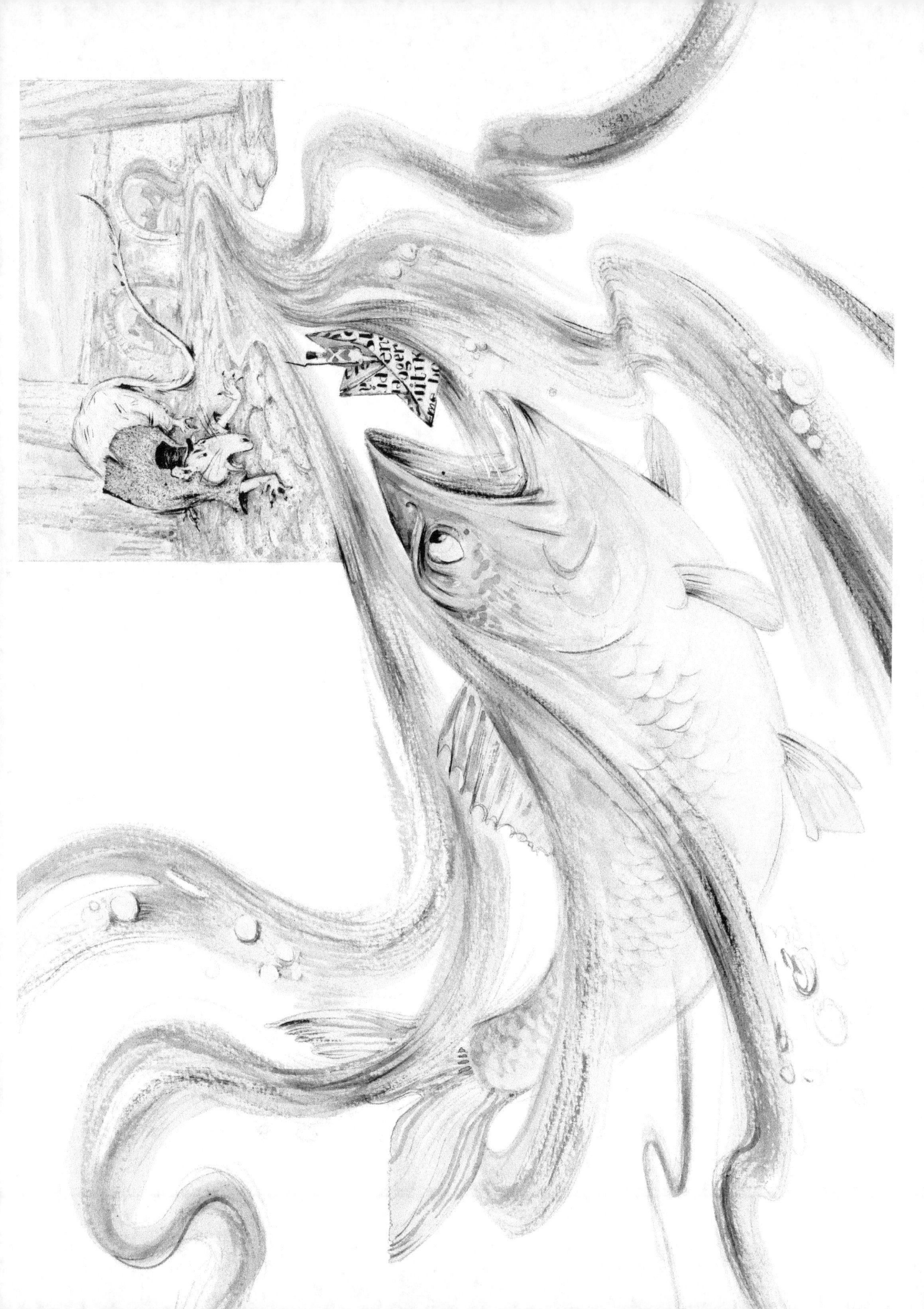

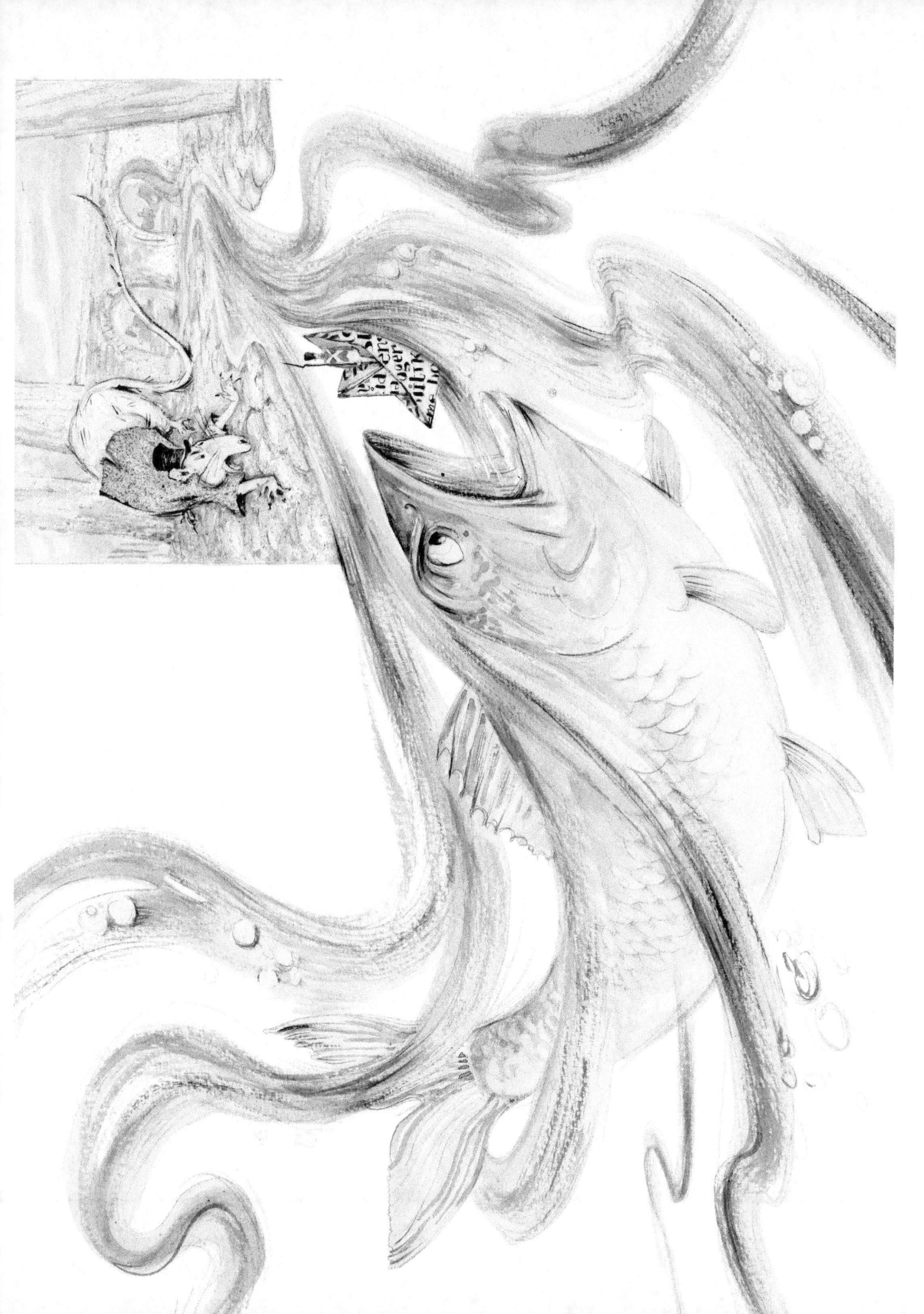

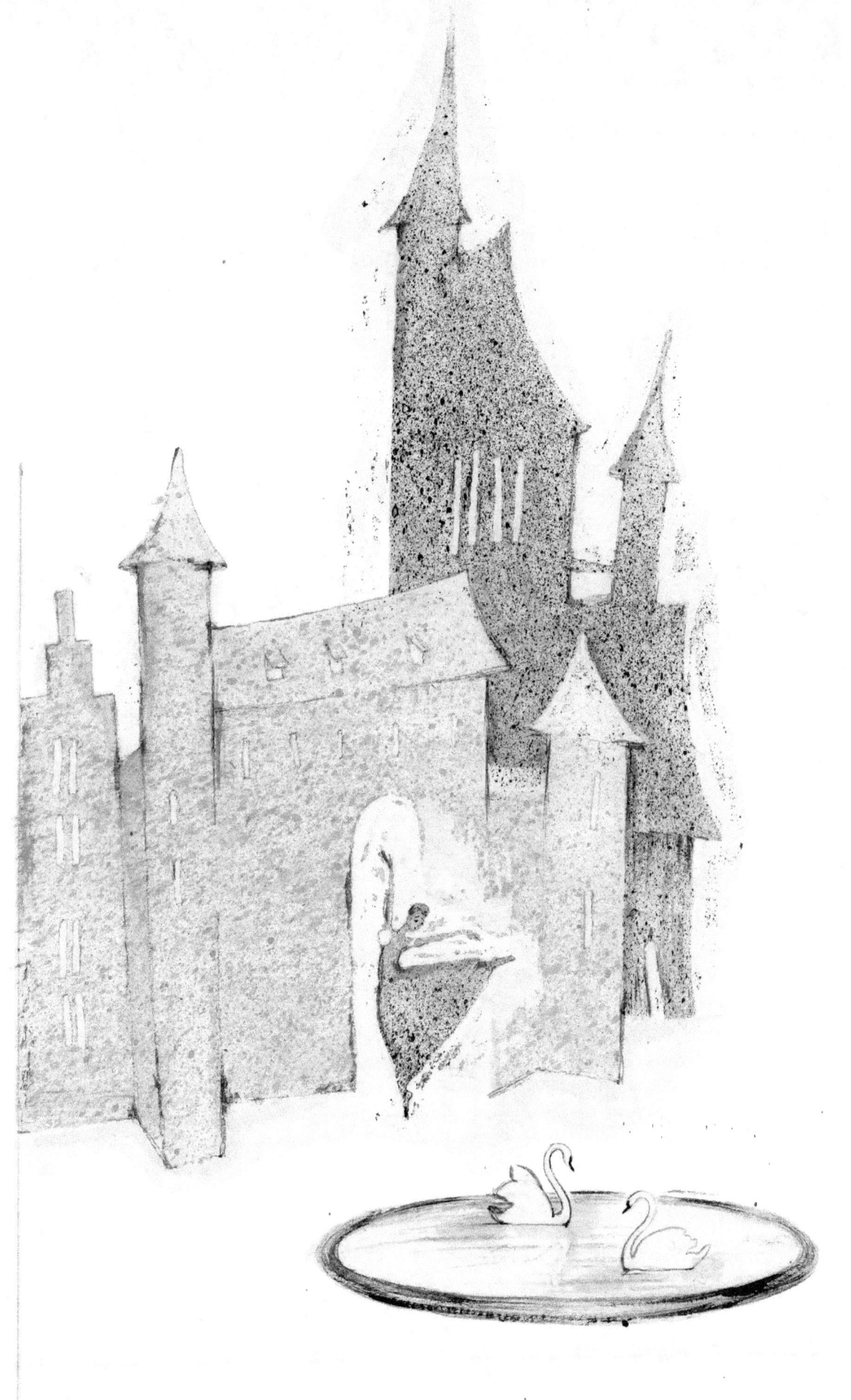

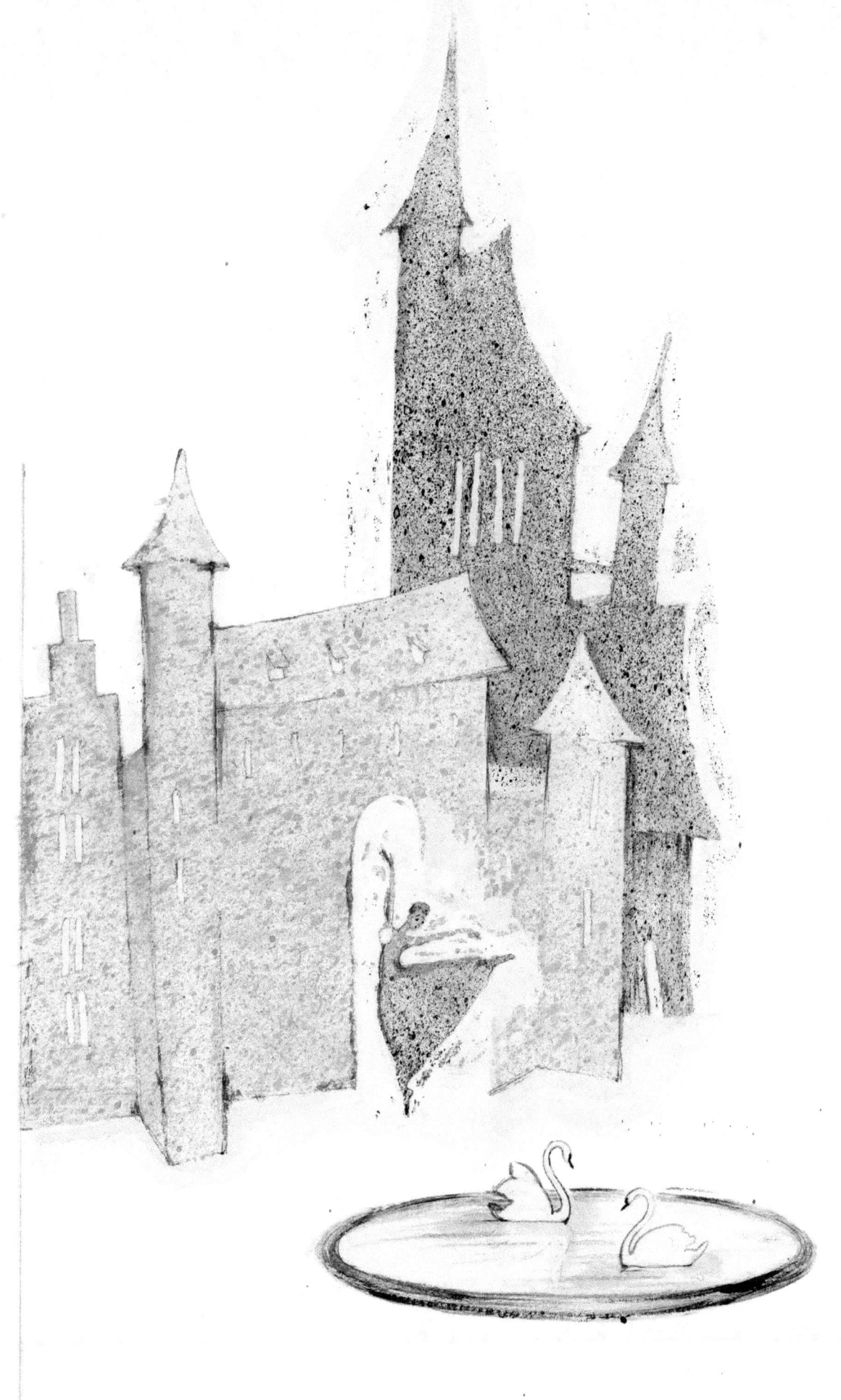

www.ingramcontent.com/pod-product-compliance
Lightning Source LLC
Chambersburg PA
CBHW080303180526
45167CB00006B/2654

9781543142518